WALES

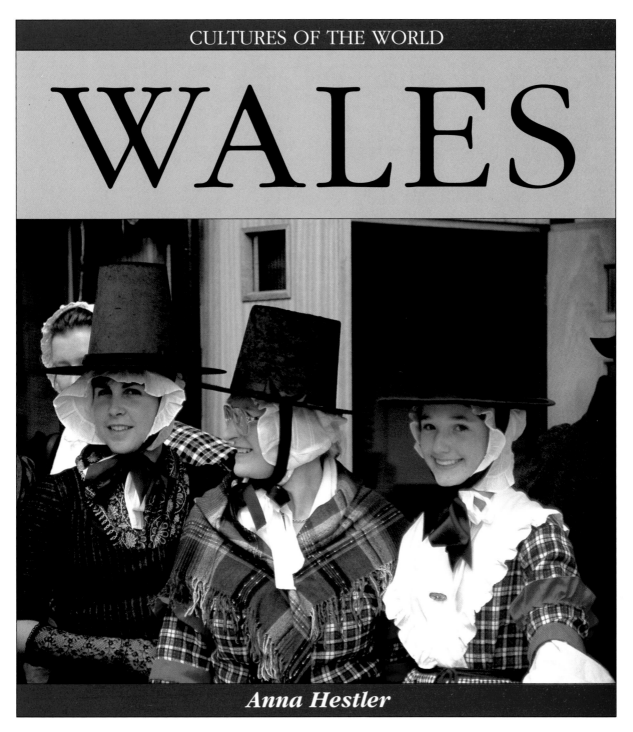

Anna Hestler

MARSHALL CAVENDISH
New York • London • Sydney

Reference edition reprinted 2001 by
Marshall Cavendish Corporation
99 White Plains Road
Tarrytown
New York 10591

© Times Media Private Limited 2001

Originated and designed by
Times Books International, an imprint of
Times Media Private Limited, a member of the
Times Publishing Group

∫P3 α∫?/

Printed in Malaysia

Library of Congress Cataloging-in-Publication Data:

Hestler, Anna.
  Wales / Anna Hestler.
    p. cm. — (Cultures of the world)
  Includes bibliographical references and index.
  ISBN 0-7614-1195-X
  1. Wales—Juvenile literature. [1. Wales.] I. Title. II. Series.

DA708.H47 2001
942.9—dc21
                              00-047426
                                CIP
                                 AC

INTRODUCTION

AS SOON AS YOU ENTER WALES FROM ENGLAND, you know you are in a different country. The road signs are bilingual, and they lead to strange sounding places like Aberystwyth and Llandudno. This is Cymru ("COME-ri"), which is the Welsh name for the country. Wales is part of the United Kingdom, but it has its own distinct culture, rooted in an ancient Celtic past.

This proud nation has been invaded many times, but it has managed to preserve its identity through an ancient tradition of poetry, legend, and song. This is a land where you will see medieval castles and be told tales of lost heroes, fire-breathing dragons, and mysterious wizards. This is a land where traditional festivals of poetry and song are held alongside modern rock concerts. But most of all this is a land with a warm and welcoming spirit. As the Welsh would say in their own language, "*Croeso i Gymru*" ("KROY-so-e-Kum-ri")—"Welcome to Wales."

CONTENTS

Ticket-seller for the Bala Lake Railway.

CONTENTS

A statue of the Welsh poet Dylan Thomas in Swansea, his hometown.

GEOGRAPHY

WALES, A SMALL BUT BEAUTIFUL COUNTRY, has a total land area of 8,019 square miles (20,768 square km), about the size of the state of New Jersey. It is part of Great Britain, which also comprises England and Scotland, and is surrounded by water on three sides: the Irish Sea on the north, St. George's Channel and Cardigan Bay on the west, and the Bristol Channel on the south. The only land border is on the east with England. The landscape in Wales is remarkably diverse, and the weather much like the rest of Great Britain—cool summers, mild winters, and lots of rain!

NORTH WALES

Colorful seashores, big beaches, green hills, and rugged peaks—North Wales has it all. The highest mountains are to be found in Snowdonia

Left: **Llanberis Pass in Snowdonia National Park.**

Opposite: **Snowdon in the evening, reflected in the calm waters of Llyn Padarn.**

Wales is made of rocks that are hundreds of millions of years old and includes materials from the Cambrian, Ordovician, and Silurian periods. The oldest rocks, however, are found on the Isle of Anglesey in the north. From the Pre-Cambrian period, these rocks are over 3.9 billion years old.

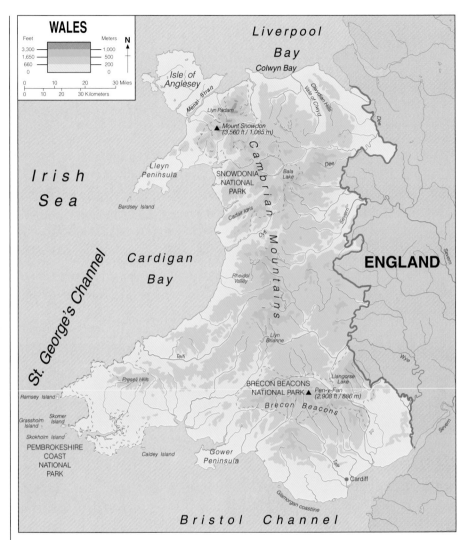

WALES

Feet	Meters
3,300	1,000
1,650	500
660	200
0	0

N

0   10   20   30 Miles
0   10   20   30 Kilometers

Liverpool Bay

Colwyn Bay

Isle of Anglesey

Menai Strait

Llyn Padarn

▲ Mount Snowdon
(3,560 ft / 1,085 m)

Clwydian Hills

Vale of Clwyd

Dee

Irish Sea

Lleyn Peninsula

SNOWDONIA NATIONAL PARK

Bala Lake

Dee

Cambrian Mountains

Bardsey Island

Cader Idris

Severn

Cardigan Bay

St. George's Channel

Rheidol Valley

ENGLAND

Severn

Llyn Brianne

Teifi

Preseli Hills

Llangorse Lake

Ramsey Island

BRECON BEACONS NATIONAL PARK ▲ Pen-y-Fan
(2,908 ft / 886 m)

Brecon Beacons

Wye

Grassholm Island

Skomer Island

Skokholm Island

PEMBROKESHIRE COAST NATIONAL PARK

Caldey Island

Gower Peninsula

Taff

Severn

Cardiff

Glamorgan coastline

Bristol Channel

National Park, named after Mount Snowdon, the highest mountain in England and Wales, standing at 3,561 feet (1,085 m). This was the training ground for the first successful expedition to climb Mount Everest.

Farther south, the peak of Cader Idris looms into view. To the northeast, rising above the lush Vale of Clwyd are the smooth Clwydian Hills, a natural barrier between England and Wales. Off the northwest coast, the Isle of Anglesey is separated from the mainland by the Menai Strait, but is joined by two bridges. Just below Anglesey, the Lleyn Peninsula juts into the Irish Sea.

MID-WALES

Mid-Wales runs from the Dyfi River to the mouth of the Teifi River and east to the border with England. It contains part of Snowdonia National Park and a sliver of the Brecon Beacons. Mid-Wales is an area of tranquil beauty—a blend of green fields, gentle hills, majestic mountains, and sweeping shores.

The ancient and austere slopes of the Cambrian Mountains are frequented by climbers and trekkers. Those who prefer the sea head west to the coast along Cardigan Bay, an area with beaches and charming towns like Aberystwyth, a lively university town. Farther down the coast, the town of New Quay has a hospital for sea birds and marine creatures. Inland, there are remote lakes, waterfalls, and cool forests that offer wonderful woodland walks.

A solitary climber stands spellbound on a summit in Snowdonia.

SOUTH AND WEST WALES

This region extends from the leafy Wye Valley on the border with England to the western tip of Pembrokeshire. This spectacular area is full of unexpected contrasts, including two very different national parks—Pembrokeshire Coast and Brecon Beacons. The Pembrokeshire Coast National Park is Britain's only coastal park and is full of rare wildlife and spectacular flowers. The Welsh national flower, the yellow daffodil, grows freely in the charming seaside town of Tenby. The gentle Preseli Hills, not too far away, are shrouded in mystery because the stones that make up the inner circle of Stonehenge were quarried here. Nobody is quite sure how they were transported to England.

Handsome, colorful Georgian houses overlook the harbor of Tenby, one of Wales' premier resorts.

SEA EMPRESS SPILL

It is not every day that a small country like Wales makes headlines around the world. However, in February 1996 it did. Newspapers were awash with the news of an ecological disaster: the oil tanker *Sea Empress* had spilled 76,000 tons of oil into the sea just off the Pembrokeshire coast.

A major clean-up operation of the rocks and oil-covered beaches ensued to minimize the damage to tourism. But the environment will take longer to restore. The spill killed an entire population of rare starfish, and it will be years before the ecological system returns to normal.

Inland, the Brecon Beacons National Park is gorgeous, with wide-open spaces and grassy summits. When English novelist Daniel Defoe came to visit in the 17th century, he said, "The English call it Breakneckshire, 'tis mountainous to the extremity." The classic walk in the park is to the top of Pen-y-Fan, the highest point in southern Wales at 2,908 feet (886 m). Although the southern mountains look enticing, they can be quite foreboding when brisk winds combine with heavy mists and rain. It is no wonder the Brecon Beacons are used as a training ground for the army.

The southern coast is more industrialized, but there are still fine stretches of natural beauty, such as the breezy Gower Peninsula and the Glamorgan Heritage Coast, which has some mountainous dunes that contain medieval villages that gradually became covered in sand. Much of the beauty of the valleys in southern Wales was scarred by the coal industry, but the area is now returning to its past splendor, thanks to the government's land reclamation program.

The town of Tintern nestles in the charming Wye Valley.

RIVERS AND LAKES

Wales has many rivers, streams, and lakes, and some offer excellent fishing opportunities. The longest rivers are the Dee, Severn, and Wye, which flow through the lowlands along the English border. The Severn, which empties into the Bristol Channel, is one of the longest rivers in England and Wales. The Wye is a great salmon river, and the surrounding area was a source of inspiration for the poet William Wordsworth.

There are many lovely lakes, including Bala Lake in northern Wales. This is the largest natural lake in Wales. It is a popular spot for water sports and home to a unique fish called a *gwyniad* ("GWIN-yad"), which is related to the salmon. Llangorse Lake is the largest natural lake in the south. According to legend, this lake covers an ancient city. It is known for certain that lake dwellers used to live on an artificial island that can still be seen from the shore.

Wales also has a number of artificial lakes, waterways, and reservoirs. Llyn Brianne, a reservoir which serves the southwest, was built with the protection of the natural environment in mind. A special fish trap was constructed below its dam to trap salmon swimming upstream to spawn. The salmon are then collected and driven beyond the dam in a van equipped with a special breathing tank. The Monmouthshire and Brecon Canal, built in 1812, was used to transport raw materials between Brecon and Newport and is now popular with leisure boaters.

FLORA

About 5,000 years ago, Wales was covered in oak forests. Although pockets of woodland remain, most of the forests have disappeared due to forest clearance and overgrazing, which has prevented regrowth. Much of Wales is now covered by induced grassland and plantation woodland, and dominated by conifers, which provide timber but not a welcoming habitat for birds and animals. Pengelli Forest in Pembrokeshire, home to both English Midland hawthorn and oak trees, is the most representative of the ancient Welsh forests.

Sea campion in bloom on Skokholm Island. This is one of the most common plants to be found along the Welsh coastline, due to its resistance to sea spray.

Wales has many beautiful wild plants and flowers. Vivid violet sea lavender and white water lilies can be found around the freshwater lakes. The coastal sand dunes support marram grass, sea holly, and evening primroses. Delicate purple saxifrages decorate the slopes of the Brecon Beacons. The white Snowdon lily carpets the slopes of Mount Snowdon, but it can only be seen in late May and early June.

Many of the islands off southern Wales are official nature reserves. Because of their exposure to harsh winds, the vegetation is largely shrubby heath and herb-rich grassland. The largest and most accessible island is Skomer Island, which has colorful rock gardens with red campion. To its south lies Skokholm Island, where purple-red rocks are smothered with spongy lichen. Apart from these islands, there are five Areas of Outstanding Natural Beauty in Wales—the Gower Peninsula, the Lleyn Peninsula, the Isle of Anglesey, the Clywdian Range, and the Wye Valley.

Both Skomer and Skokholm islands have colonies of guillemots, razorbills, storm petrels, kittiwakes, and puffins.

FAUNA

The Welsh coastline has some of the best seabird breeding colonies in Europe. One of the world's largest gannet colonies is on Grassholm Island, with 30,000 pairs of these magnificent white birds. Ramsey Island is home to a rare chough, and 30% of the Manx shearwater population lives on Bardsey Island. Bardsey Island used to be a place of pilgrimage and is said to be the burial place of 20,000 holy men.

Inland, the hills and the valleys are alive with birdsong. Mid-Wales is home to the red kite. These graceful, reddish birds of prey nearly became extinct in the 1930s. Since then, a great deal of effort has been made to protect them, but there are still only about 150 breeding pairs. Two other endangered birds—the merlin and the dipper—also live in the hills of Wales.

A closeup of the gannets on Grassholm Island. These birds spend most of their lives above water and dive with half-closed wings to catch fish and squid.

Wales is also home to a range of mammals. The pine marten, which resembles a cat, lives in the wooded mountains and hills, and black-eyed polecats are found around Snowdonia and along the coastal dunes. The Welsh pony is a familiar sight in the foothills, as are wild goats on the harsh mountain slopes. Skomer Island has a special island species of vole, and along the rocky coast, ringed seals bask in the sunshine.

CITIES AND TOWNS

CARDIFF is the capital city of Wales, but it is not a particularly Welsh city. One is more likely to hear English than Welsh spoken here, and the population is one of the most cosmopolitan in Wales.

The history of Cardiff goes back to the Romans, who built forts along the Taff River. At the beginning of the 19th century, it was no more than a small town. It grew to become the world's busiest coal-exporting port by 1913, due to its proximity to the southern coal and iron mines. At the height of the coal boom, dozens of ships were anchored just outside the port waiting their turn to enter. But the coal trade began to decline after

Swansea, Wales' maritime city, is justly proud of its 600-berth marina. The Maritime Museum is the building in the center.

World War I, and recently the docks were closed. The city is now dedicated to commerce and administration. The Cardiff Bay Redevelopment Corporation is also redeveloping the entire waterfront as a tourist area.

Cardiff Castle sits in the heart of the city. Originally a Roman fort, it was later enlarged by the Normans, then renovated in 1872 by William Burges, with the fortune of the third Marquess of Bute. Cardiff also has an elegant Edwardian civic center, built in 1904. The civic buildings are of white Portland cement and include the City Hall, Law Courts, the National Museum of Wales, the Welsh Office, and the Temple of Peace and Health.

SWANSEA is the second largest city in Wales. The poet Dylan Thomas, who was born here, described it as "an ugly, lovely town." It does have a lovely location on the bay, but it used to be the center of the copper industry and became terribly polluted. Much of the city center was bombed during World War II but has since been rebuilt.

Today the city is a much nicer place to live. It has a modern shopping center, the oldest museum in Wales, and the remains of an old castle.

The Guildhall contains the city's main concert hall and an impressive display of murals by Sir Frank Brangwyn, a Welsh artist. A lot of attention has been directed to the waterfront. The old docklands have been rejuvenated, and there is a huge marina and a Maritime and Industrial Museum with a working woolen mill. A footpath runs along the bay to Mumbles, a quaint seaside resort.

ABERYSTWYTH is located on the beautiful Cardigan Bay and is considered the capital of Mid-Wales. It is a university town, a seaside resort, and the headquarters of the Welsh Language Society. The university campus contains an arts center and the National Library of Wales. This library has some of the oldest surviving books and manuscripts in Wales, such as *The Black Book of Carmarthen*, the oldest book written in Welsh.

Constitution Hill, a steep outcrop on the northern end of the town, can be reached by riding the electric Cliff Railway, built in 1896. Its summit boasts a view of the whole town, from which can be seen the remains of an Iron Age fort and Aberystwyth Castle, built in 1277 by Edward I.

The old University College of Wales, with its mock-Gothic tower, is now the University Theological College. Beyond it lie the pier and promenade, as well as the Cliff Railway on Constitution Hill.

HISTORY

THROUGHOUT THE COURSE of their history, the Welsh have struggled against invaders: the Romans, the Saxons, the Vikings, and the Normans. However, Wales finally lost its independence when it was united with England under the Acts of Union (1536 and 1543).

EARLY INHABITANTS

The earliest inhabitants were hunters and gatherers, and there is little evidence that many settlements or monuments existed before 4,000 B.C. However, about 4,000 B.C., Neolithic peoples arrived from the western coasts of Europe and introduced farming to Wales. They used stone tools and lived in simple houses. They also built great communal graves, which were either stone tombs concealed under mounds of rubble or long barrows. These stone tombs were probably the burial chambers of important families, some containing elaborately decorated stones, and about 150 of them have been found in Wales. There are also signs that their settlements were attacked and burned in violent wars.

From 2,300 B.C. onwards, people of the Bronze Age arrived from central and northwestern Europe, bringing with them skills in metalwork and more sophisticated bronze tools. They were known as the "Beaker People" because of the way they buried their dead. They laid the bodies out in stone-lined graves alongside various objects, such as a small clay beaker. It is possible that this beaker contained a special drink associated with the burial ritual.

Above: **St. Brynach's Cross—a pre-Norman Celtic cross.**

Opposite: **The 13th-century gateway of Monnow Bridge at Monmouth.**

19

THE CELTS

The Celts were early Indo-European people who spread over much of Europe from 2,000 B.C. to 100 B.C. In Britain these migrants included the Dumnoii in Cornwall, the Dobuni on the upper Thames, and the Ordovices in Wales. After Rome conquered Gaul in around 55 B.C., significant numbers of Gallic and Belgic tribespeople also emigrated to Britain.

The Celts were a people who loved war and adventure, music, pleasure, and feasts. An advanced people, they were weavers, potters, and skilled metalworkers. Their art characteristically used abstract geometric designs and stylized bird and animal forms.

Believing that their gods communicated with the druids (a priestly caste with secret knowledge of sacred rituals), the Celts had a polytheistic religion that involved human sacrifice, usually in the form of burning men alive. The spirits of the woods, rivers, sea, and sky were holy to the Celts. Especially important were the spirits of springs and lakes. Some of these were thought to possess healing powers, while others had the power to grant favors. The modern custom of throwing coins in a fountain for luck may have developed from these Celtic beliefs.

CELTIC WARRIORS

The Celts were fierce warriors, remarkable for their height, muscularity, and fair coloring. They often painted themselves with blue dye to terrify their opponents in battle. Using a variety of weapons such as iron swords, spears, daggers, and wooden shields, they also rode horse-drawn chariots that were fast and agile. During battle, they often hurled javelins and sometimes jumped down from their horses to fight on foot.

No doubt the Romans must have thought twice as they prepared to attack Anglesey, the stronghold of the druids. The Roman historian Tacitus gives a descriptive account of the Celts: "The enemy lined the shores with a dense armed mass. Among them were black-robed women with disheveled hair, like Furies brandishing torches. Close by stood druids, raising their hands to heaven and screaming dreadful curses...At this sight our soldiers were gripped by fear." But the Romans did not retreat. Instead, they crossed the strait, slaughtered the druids, and destroyed their holy altars. They defeated the Celts by around 58 B.C.

THE ROMANS

Julius Caesar invaded England around 55 B.C. Despite opposition from Welsh tribes led by Caradog (or Caratacus to the Romans), Roman conquest was complete by A.D. 78. The Romans built military camps and set up towns such as Cardiff and Carmarthen.

They also constructed roads and a great highway called Sarn Helen joining North and South Wales. There are different theories about the origins of this name. Some say that the name of the highway comes from Sarn y Lleng, the Causeway of the Legions. Others say it means "Helen's Causeway" and was named after Helen, the wife of Magnus Maximus, who was the Roman commander at that time. Roman troops traveled up and down this highway, transporting the lead, copper, iron, silver, and gold that they had mined in Wales.

Although the Romans occupied Wales for more than 300 years, they never managed to conquer all of it. Wales was never fully Romanized, and many of its people continued their traditional way of life. By about A.D. 400, increasing pressure from numerous invading tribes and domestic threats forced the Romans to relinquish their control of Britain.

The Celts were skillful metalworkers and used iron sickles to cut their crops. They made soup in large cauldrons that were hung on cords and tied to the roofs of their homes. The soup was made from vegetables such as peas and beans, and sometimes oats and barley were added.

Opposite: **An ancient Celtic warrior in traditional dress—a tunic covered by a cloak, which is fastened by a brooch.**

A hand-colored woodcut of Roman soldiers in combat.

THE DARK AGES

After the Romans left, Britain entered the Dark Ages—so named because of the disintegration of Romanic Britain, and because only fragments of information survive from this age. Raids by neighbors were commonplace, and by the beginning of the fourth century A.D., the Scots had invaded from the west, the Picts from the far north, and seafaring Germanic tribes, the Angles, Saxons, and Jutes from the southeast. This period marked the beginning of early Welsh political organization, as Britain became carved up into small warring kingdoms.

This was also a time of consolidation for Christiandom. The Romans had introduced Christianity, but it was spread at this time by traveling "saints" who converted others to the faith, which is how the Dark Ages in Wales became known as the Age of Saints. One of these saints, Dewi (or David), became the patron saint of Wales.

Towards the end of the sixth century A.D., pagan Saxon tribes advanced steadily into Britain. They began a struggle that continued until Henry VII took the throne 900 years later. Their advance was temporarily checked by a great victory, led by a certain Briton—Ambrosius Aurelianus, over the Anglo-Saxons at a place called Mons Badonicus. Little else is known about this hero, but he lives on in legend as King Arthur. Nevertheless this was a short-lived victory, and the Saxons continued pushing northwards and westwards.

In the eighth century A.D., Offa, the greatest king of the Anglo-Saxon kingdom of Mercia, built a long dike to define the territory of his kingdom, and the border between England and Wales has been defined by it ever since.

An artist's impression of King Arthur's legendary "Round Table," hanging on the wall of Winchester Cathedral.

THE NINTH AND TENTH CENTURIES

Throughout the ninth and tenth centuries, Wales was attacked many times by Norse pirates (Vikings) who came from Scandinavia. However, the Vikings never succeeded in colonizing Wales, partly because of Rhodri Mawr (Roderick the Great) who ruled most of Wales, with the exception of the extreme southwest and southeast. (His grandson, Hywel Dda, is remembered for introducing a code of law that survived until the arrival of Edward I.)

By the tenth century, with the help of Welsh kings, King Alfred of Wessex had recovered all control from the Danes and forced them out of Great Britain.

Scene of a Norse raid.

THE NORMAN CONQUEST

Under the leadership of William the Conqueror, the Normans, who came from France, defeated the Anglo-Saxons in England at the Battle of Hastings in 1066. In order to secure his conquest, William the Conqueror made a pact with Welsh rulers recognizing their authority in their own kingdoms. In the borderlands, called the Marches, Norman lords were given extensive powers as "marcher lords" to keep the local population under control. Meanwhile, from Chester and Shrewsbury, the Normans penetrated farther into Wales. By 1093 the Normans had invaded almost all of southern Wales, including Cardigan, Pembroke, Brecon, and Glamorgan.

The Normans founded market towns, where livestock sales still take place today. They were also great castle-builders. Although the Normans managed to colonize the lowlands of South and Mid-Wales, the Welsh language and culture remained strong in the northern highlands. In North Wales the three Welsh kingdoms of Gwynedd, Powys, and Deheubarth

At about 9 a.m. on October 14, 1066, William I, Duke of Normandy, engaged his 7,000-strong Norman army against a similar-sized English force. William's troops pretended to flee, drawing the English after them. They then turned around and picked the pursuers off one by one, earning William the English crown and the title "the Conqueror."

The battle scene in 1275 during which Llewllyn the Last, Prince of Wales (1224–82), was defeated by English troops.

regained power from the Normans by the 12th century.

Literature flourished at this time. *The History of Gruffydd ap Cynan,* by Welsh historian Giraldus Cambrensis, revealed the political and cultural values of Wales during the time of the first king of Gwynedd—Gruffydd ap Cynan. Many epic poems, romances, and legends were also recorded for the first time. The oldest book in Welsh is the *Black Book of Carmarthen,* a book containing the work of court poets and produced in the 12th century by Cistercian monks.

By the late 12th century, two great Welsh heroes began the struggle for Welsh independence from the English. The first was Llywelyn ap Iorwerth (Llywelyn the Great), who succeeded in ruling nearly all of North Wales. He sided with the English barons and signed the Magna Carta, obtaining some rights for Wales. However, this was a superficial alliance; when he died in 1240, the land was divided again.

Later on his grandson, Llywelyn ap Gruffudd (Llywelyn the Last), came to power and restored a degree of unity. Proclaiming himself Prince of Wales, he made a treaty in 1267 with the English king, Henry III, to recognize his title, but this peacekeeping measure failed. When Henry died in 1272, Llywelyn refused to accept

King Edward I (1272–1307) was a renowned warrior, earning the nickname "Hammer of the Scots."

his successor, Edward I of England, and led a revolt. Edward I invaded Wales in 1277 and Llywelyn was ambushed and killed on December 11, 1282. All hopes of Welsh independence were dashed. In 1284 the Statute of Rhuddlan brought the whole of Wales under the control of the English monarch and the English system of law.

ENGLAND TAKES OVER

After the defeat of Llywelyn the Last, Edward I started a program of castle-building, both for security and as a symbol of English power. The mighty Caernarfon Castle, where Edward's son (Edward II) was born and bestowed with the title Prince of Wales, still towers over the medieval town of Caernarfon. The great Conwy, Caernarfon, Harlech, and Beaumaris castles were also built during this time.

Under Edward I, Wales was administered by the English, with the Welsh in less influential positions of power. The Welsh were discontented with their subordinate position, and eventually, a nobleman named Owen Glendower led them in a rebellion that lasted nearly 14 years. In the period 1400 to 1407, the government lost control of the greater part of Wales but later managed to regain power.

In 1485 Henry Tudor (King Henry VII) ascended the English throne. The Welsh were delighted because the Tudors could trace their ancestry back to the Welsh princes. However, although Henry Tudor gave some Welshmen positions at court, he did not give much attention to Wales as a whole.

Henry Tudor's son, Henry VIII, legally united Wales with England under the Acts of Union (1536 and 1543). Under these acts, new counties were formed, and Welsh towns were given representation in the English Parliament. For the first time in history, Welshmen enjoyed the same political status as Englishmen. However, after the Acts of Union, the Welsh landowners became increasingly remote from the ordinary people who farmed their land. These landowners spoke English, identified with the English, and sent their children to school in England, thus establishing a pattern of social division in Wales.

INDUSTRIAL REVOLUTION AND METHODISM

The Industrial Revolution was a turning point in the history of Wales. New industries sprang up, and many people left rural Wales to work in the mines. Sadly the situation was not quite as they had expected, and they were often exploited. Inevitably this resulted in a great deal of social unrest, including riots, which created a fertile ground for the Methodist Revival in the 18th century, a religious movement that completely changed the social atmosphere in Wales.

Methodism had its strongest following in the mining valleys of South Wales and the factory towns of the English Midlands. An incredible number of those who converted to Methodism were largely motivated by the continued disregard for the ordinary Welsh people by the Welsh gentry and the English Parliament. It was made worse by the fact that the

Henry Tudor's granddaughter Elizabeth became Queen of England. She was a tall, striking woman with red hair who governed well and was proud of her Welsh ancestry. To ensure that Protestantism took root in Wales, she had the Bible translated into Welsh (1567 and 1588), which also helped to keep the Welsh language alive.

established church was pro-English. The Methodist Revival gave the Welsh a new sense of identity and strengthened the Welsh language.

The 19th century was a melting pot of movements. Other than religious concerns, there was also a new sense of political direction in the country. People gained a greater sense of Welshness and began a national movement for home rule. World War I had a profound effect on Welsh life. After the war, the economy went into a slump and people became less optimistic. They lost their faith and religious observance declined. By the end of the 20th century, the coal and steel industries in Wales had collapsed, causing widespread unemployment and forcing the country to redefine its future.

Young coal miners at work in the mines at Blaenavon, in North Wales, in 1939.

GOVERNMENT

WALES (CYMRU IN WELSH) IS ONE of the countries that make up Great Britain, which also includes England and Scotland. Great Britain and Northern Ireland form the United Kingdom, which is a constitutional monarchy and parliamentary democracy. The four member countries differ from each other in many cultural aspects; thus although there is one government, some aspects of local government are organized differently.

THE STRUCTURE OF GOVERNMENT

Wales is a principality with a Prince of Wales. It is governed by Whitehall, the United Kingdom's political and administrative center in London, England and by its own National Assembly in Cardiff. The United Kingdom is unusual in that it does not have a written constitution. Its governing

Left: **A Welsh girl wearing traditional costume and carrying a basket of daffodils. The Welsh word for "daffodil" is similar to "leek," which is why both have been adopted as national emblems.**

Opposite: **Demonstrators participating in a rally for a Welsh National Assembly. The Welsh Language Society's placard reads: "Freedom! Parliament for the people of Wales."**

NATIONAL EMBLEMS

Most countries have ordinary animals or birds for emblems, but Wales has a mythical beast—the dragon. This adorns the green and white background on the national flag. Nobody is quite sure how the red dragon became the emblem of Wales. One theory is that the Romans used the dragon as a military standard, and the Welsh continued this practice after the Romans left. There may be some truth to this because the English word "dragon" and the Welsh word *draig* ("DRYG") are both derived from the Latin root *draco*.

The Prince of Wales' feathers are another national emblem of Wales. The crest of ostrich plumes and the German motto: "*Homout; ich dien*" (meaning "Courage; I serve") were introduced by Edward the Black Prince (1330–76), who became Prince of Wales in 1343. These feathers currently adorn the badge of the national Welsh rugby team.

principles are a combination of parliamentary statutes, common law (legal principles based on precedents that can be traced back to Anglo-Saxon times), and convention.

The head of state is Queen Elizabeth II, but in reality, the United Kingdom is governed through parliament. Parliament consists of the queen, the House of Lords and the House of Commons, the latter being the more important of the two houses. The queen appoints the prime minister, who is the leader of the majority party in the House of Commons. All other ministers are appointed based on the advice of the prime minister. The most important ministers make up the cabinet, which works closely with the prime minister to make policy decisions. Wales elects 40 members of parliament (MPs) to the House of Commons who participate in the governing of the United Kingdom and look after the interests of their supporters in Wales.

In parliament, Welsh matters are discussed in the Welsh Grand Committee and the Welsh Affairs Committee. In 1964 a secretary of state for Wales was appointed, with a seat in the cabinet and a department in London known as the Welsh Office. The Welsh Office negotiated the overall budget for Wales and primary legislation affecting the principality. A recent move towards devolution was the creation, in 1999, of a 60-member National Assembly for Wales led by a first secretary. The Welsh Office is now part of the National Assembly, which is situated in Cardiff.

The National Assembly for Wales building at Cathays Park, Cardiff.

PRINCE OF WALES

The custom of naming the monarch's eldest son Prince of Wales began in 1284, when King Edward I bestowed this title on his son, who was born at Caernarfon Castle in northwestern Wales. The history of the title goes back to its only Welsh holder Llwelyn the Last, who was recognized as a prince in 1267.

The current Prince of Wales is Prince Charles. Most, but not all, Welsh recognize his title. On the evening before his ceremonial investiture in 1969, two Welsh men blew themselves up while planting explosives at a government office in Abergele (in south-western Wales). These were the first men to die in the name of Welsh nationalism. Later, at his investiture in Caernarfon Castle, some nationalists wore badges that said, "No English Prince is Prince of Wales."

DEVOLUTION

Various politicians have been pressing for devolution since the 19th century, and the issue has been debated within the ranks of the political parties. In 1956 Megan Lloyd George and S.O. Davies, two Welsh Labor MPs who had been pushing for more independence, presented a petition to parliament for a Welsh Assembly. As a token gesture to appease Welsh nationalists, the ruling Conservative Party appointed a part-time Welsh minister, confirmed Cardiff as the capital city of Wales in 1955, and made the Welsh flag official in 1959.

When the Labor Party won the general election in 1964, it created the post of secretary of state for Wales. Supported by a separate department known as the Welsh Office, this would give Wales a greater say within the UK government. Demands from the Welsh for an elected assembly with powers devolved from Westminister became more strident, and this led to an act giving Wales a measure of devolution in 1978. In 1979 the Welsh voted on the issue but rejected the proposal for further devolution. People on both sides of the table were wary. Welsh speakers feared being dominated by the Anglicized South; Plaid Cymru (the Welsh nationalist party) was apprehensive that it would lead to Labor Party domination; and there were concerns that devolution would damage an already fragile economy.

In the 1990s the devolution issue was back on the agenda. Devolution enthusiasts argued that it would counter excessive central government control. Their opponents argued that it might encourage conflict with the rest of the United Kingdom. The issue was finally settled by a referendum in 1997 when a slim majority voted in favor of a National Assembly for Wales.

The City Hall in Cardiff, the capital of Wales.

THE NATIONAL ASSEMBLY

The National Assembly gives the Welsh more control over their own affairs by assuming the functions of the Welsh Office and allocating the budget approved by the secretary of state for Wales. The National Assembly will also take on an economic role and promote Welsh interests in the European Union.

Unlike the Scottish Parliament, the assembly will not be able to raise taxes, and the parliament in London will still be the primary lawmaker for Wales. However, it will be able to make secondary legislation (the rules and regulations that fill in the framework set out in the Acts of Parliament). The central government will continue to be responsible for foreign affairs, defense, taxation, overall economic policy, and social security.

Ron Davies, former secretary of state for Wales, led the devolution referendum campaign, which led to a narrow "Yes" vote on September 18, 1997.

POLITICAL PARTIES IN WALES

All the main British political parties (the Labor Party, the Liberal Democrats, and the Conservatives) are active in Wales, as is Plaid Cymru. The Labor Party has a strong following among the Welsh. Prior to World War I, Welsh politics was marked by a pro-Welsh liberal tradition. During World War I, both men and women were involved in Britain's war effort, which was led by a Welsh prime minister named David Lloyd George. However, the war and its aftermath changed the political climate in Wales. At the end of the war, Wales went into an economic depression, and many people lost their jobs. The Liberal Party began losing ground, and many Welsh began voting for the Labor Party, which stood for nationwide solidarity and the advance of the working class. This shift was particularly noticeable in the industrialized south. The Liberal Party remained popular in parts of rural Wales, but eventually attitudes became predominantly Labor.

A Welsh woman leaving a Welsh Assembly Referendum polling station.

DAVID LLOYD GEORGE (1863–1945)

David Lloyd George is perhaps the most famous Welsh politician. He was born to Welsh parents and raised in a small village in North Wales. He was charismatic and eloquent, which made him popular with voters and winsome to women. The media nicknamed him the "Welsh Wizard" because of his full cloak, wide-brimmed hat, flowing hair, full mustache, and twinkling eyes.

His achievements were many, including laying the foundations for the welfare state and leading Great Britain to victory in World War I by reorganizing the munitions industry. During the course of his political career, Lloyd George was a Liberal Minister of Parliament, Chancellor of the Exchequer, and prime minister of England from 1916 to 1922. Toward the end of his life, he was made an earl.

Plaid Cymru's posters on a shop window.

NATIONALISM AND PLAID CYMRU

In 1925 a group of academics headed by Saunders Lewis established the Welsh Nationalist Party, or Plaid Cymru. Currently committed to achieving political independence for Wales as an independent "region" within the European Economic Community, in its early days its central aim was to protect the Welsh language. It was seen more as a pressure group and made little headway until the by-elections of 1966 when Gwynfor Evans won the first Plaid Cymru seat in parliament. This moved the party beyond the issue of language into mainstream politics where it became a non-conservative alternative to the Labor Party.

Plaid Cymru's support has always been strongest in the rural Welsh-speaking areas of central and western Wales. In recent years leaders of the party have pushed for votes outside the traditional areas, increasing the party's following. The party's philosophy has also developed in a more outward-looking and European direction. There are other movements on the periphery of Plaid Cymru; some striving for independence based on cultural and linguistic differentiation. Some of these movements, such as the Welsh Language Society and Meibion Glyndwr, have resorted to using various methods of civil disobedience.

Royal Welsh Fusiliers
on parade.

JUSTICE AND THE LAW

Wales has the same system of justice as England, and there are two kinds of courts. Most cases are dealt with by Magistrates' Court, and every town has one of these. Magistrates (or Justices of Peace) are not usually trained lawyers but are appointed by a local committee. A panel of magistrates can decide whether someone is guilty of a crime and can also impose punishment. Even serious crimes are first heard in Magistrates' Court before they are referred to a higher court, which in most cases is a Crown Court where the judge is a professional lawyer and there is a jury of 12 people who decide on a verdict. There is also a Court of Appeal to which a convicted person can apply, and the highest court in Britain is the House of Lords.

Police services are the responsibility of Whitehall but are operated and administered through local police forces. There are approximately 6,400 policemen in Wales. Although Wales does not have any independent defense arrangements, it does have three army regiments—the Welsh Guards, the Royal Welsh Fusiliers, and the Royal Regiment of Wales.

SMALLEST HOUSE →

The Smallest
House
IN GREAT BRITAIN
ADMISSION 20p

Dim o gwbl
1 Ebr-30 Medi
At any time
1 Apr-30 Sept

Dim o gwbl
At any time

ECONOMY

DURING THE 18TH AND 19TH CENTURIES, the Welsh economy moved from dependence on agriculture to dependence on heavy industry, particularly coal mining. In the second half of the 20th century, the coal industry collapsed, causing large-scale unemployment and forcing the economy to restructure. Heavy industry has all but disappeared, and Wales now has a more modern economy, dominated by high technology manufacturing and services.

INDUSTRY IN THE PAST

Prior to the 18th century, most Welsh made their living by farming, and the woolen trade was one of the most bustling. Britain's Industrial Revolution had a profound effect on the economy of Wales. The workforce shifted from farming to factory-based industries, and from rural to industrial areas. Southwestern Wales became an important center for

Left: **The end of a work shift at a Merthyr Vale colliery before its closure in 1989.**

Opposite: **This fisherman's cottage in the town of Conwy is a favorite tourist attraction. It is said to be smallest house in Britain, standing just over 10 feet (3 m) high.**

A worker applies the finishing touches to a slate tile.

the copper industry, while the valleys in South Wales (particularly Merthyr Tydfil) had some of the largest iron works. In the northeast and northwest of Wales, iron, copper, slate, and lead were mined.

Between 1840 and 1920, valleys in South Wales produced vast quantities of coal, which became the dominant industry, although steel and tin were also important. Wales became a major exporter of coal, and the Rhondda Valley became world-renowned. A steady production of coal was maintained until the 1950s, when the availability of substitutes and cheaper imports made the coal pits uneconomical. From the 1960s onwards, the pits began to close. The last pit in the Rhondda Valley closed in 1990. Today coal mining and slate quarrying have disappeared, although Wales is still an important center for steel.

INDUSTRY TODAY

To combat the negative effects of the collapse of the coal industry, the government developed a policy to encourage new industries such as engineering, manufacturing, and car assembly, to set up shop in Wales. This policy has been successful, and more recently, manufacturing and services have become the most important sectors of the economy, with tourism as one of the fastest growing. Growth in the service sector has been especially significant in banking, finance, business services, and self-employment. The growth in manufacturing has been facilitated by foreign investment.

Not all areas of the economy have grown equally well. In an attempt to spread prosperity, the Welsh Development Agency gives grants and advice to help small and medium-sized enterprises start up on their own. Some of these, like the Laura Ashley Company, have become world-famous multinational corporations.

Metal products, automotive components, and optical fibers are some of the goods manufactured in Wales, and electronics is one of the main areas of growth.

LAURA ASHLEY

Laura Mountney was born in 1925 in Merthyr Tydfil, South Wales. Her family moved to London, but Laura was sent back to Wales to escape the air raids during World War II. In 1949 she married and became Laura Ashley.

While a secretary in London, she started designing her own floral patterns, and printed them on tea towels with a printing machine designed by her husband. Many people liked her towels, so she moved back to Wales and opened a factory in Machynlleth in 1963. As her business expanded, she began making long dresses with flower patterns and opened more factories. Before long, Laura had opened shops throughout the United Kingdom, France, the United States, and Australia. She died tragically in 1985 when she fell down some stairs, but her creative talent lives on in her designs, which are still sold around the world.

Wales is known as a mecca for narrow-gauge railway enthusiasts.

TOURISM

Tourism is a flourishing sector of the economy because of the country's natural beauty and the lure of its castles and legends. There are rugged mountains, cool forests, mysterious lakes, a wonderful coastline, and countless quaint towns. Wales has everything a nature lover could want. There are plenty of hiking trails, and the national parks offer a range of activities like climbing, canoeing, and ponytrekking.

Historical sites are also good business, attracting tourists from all over the world. Apart from museums, there are over 100 impressive castles to explore, as well as Roman forts and settlements, Christian monasteries, and the remains of a romantic Celtic past. Many of these places are preserved by the Welsh Historic Monuments organization.

Visitors can also relive the past by riding on one of the "Great Little Trains," narrow-gauge steam railways that chug through some of the most scenic parts of the countryside. Many of these trains are more than 100 years old and once transported coal and slate. Even abandoned mines now attract visitors with an interest in industrial archaeology. At the Big Pit at Blaenavon and at the Rhondda Heritage Park, ex-miners show tourists how the mines once worked and tell them gripping tales of the past. Over nine million tourists visit Wales every year to enjoy its beauty and way of life.

FARMING

About four-fifths of the land in Wales is devoted to agriculture. There are many small family farms, but livestock farming accounts for about 85% of their output because of the climate and poor soil conditions.

Farmers in the highland areas rear cattle and sheep, while the lowlands are dairy farming country. On arable land farmers grow wheat, barley, oats, vegetables, and potatoes. Pembrokeshire, in the southwest, has particularly good land. It is often called the "Garden of Wales" because one can buy almost anything there from honey and ice cream to potatoes.

The agricultural sector has contracted in recent years, and farmers have had to adapt. One of the reasons for this is the increasing value of the pound against other European currencies, which has curbed exports of Welsh products and stimulated cheaper imports.

Sheep shearing is an art handed down from generation to generation. The men at this sheep shearing championship, held at Harlech, are competing to remove the wool in a complete piece in the fastest time.

FISHING AND FORESTRY

Fishing has become a relatively minor economic activity, but the Welsh coastline continues to provide an income for fishermen. The South shores are abundant with cockles, which women used to sell door-to-door in the villages. Inland, in the southwest, people used to fish from coracles, boats light enough for fishermen to carry home. These boats are still used to fish for salmon in the Teifi River, and some villages hold coracle races in summer.

Many of the forests in Wales are planted and managed by the Forestry Commission. Most of the trees, such as the dark green conifers, have been

Coracle racing, unique to Wales, can be seen on the Teifi River. These light boats are still used for salmon fishing today.

planted for timber and do not provide a natural habitat for birds and animals. After public debate, more consideration is now being given to preserving the environment. In some areas the majestic old oak, ash, and beech trees have been preserved. Oak trees along the scenic Cwm-carn Forest Drive, near Newport, have been sculpted into characters from the *Mabinogion*, a book of Welsh folklore. There is a 20-feet-tall (6-m) sculpture of the "King of Giants," which is used in storytelling sessions for the local primary schoolchildren.

WORKING

At just over 6%, the unemployment rate in 1997 was about half what it was in 1987. Over the past decade, increased employment opportunities in manufacturing, services, and through self-employment have offset job losses in heavy industry.

The workforce is concentrated in the industrial areas in the south and northeast of Wales. As the economy continues to move away from farming, Wales faces the problem of rural depopulation. To combat this, the government is trying to attract young people back to rural areas. The Development Board for Rural Wales was set up in 1977 to attract businesses to Mid-Wales.

There was an influx of women into the workforce during the two World Wars when women took over traditionally "male" jobs in the factories, while the men were away at war. During the consumer boom of the 1950s and 1960s, more jobs became available for women. There was also an increasing acceptance of a woman's dual role as wife and mother and career woman. However, although more women are working, they still, on average, earn less than men and are under-represented in management.

By the end of the 19th century, over a quarter of a million men worked in the coal mines of the valleys in South Wales. The Rhondda Valley alone employed 40,000. During the 1980s and 1990s, pit closures caused massive unemployment and disrupted entire communities.

47

Shops along a street in Carmarthen.

SHOPPING

In Wales the "High Street" is usually the main shopping area in towns and cities. Most large towns have major supermarkets, such as Tesco, and department stores, such as Marks and Spencer. In recent years there has been an increase in the number of big supermarkets built on the outskirts of larger towns and cities. These cater to the increasing consumer demand for one-stop shopping and carry everything from food to housewares and from clothing to hardware. However, shopping habits in smaller villages have changed less quickly, and people are still more likely to buy from their local butcher and baker.

Most neighborhoods have a corner shop. Corner shops sell some food, but their main business is selling newspapers, cigarettes, candy, and other conveniences. On Sunday people will pop out to the corner shop to pick up the newspaper and a quart of milk. Shopkeepers usually know their local customers by name and enjoy chatting with them.

TRANSPORTATION

Highways and bridges link the major industrial and residential centers in Great Britain. The Severn Bridge is the gateway to South Wales from England. When it was built in 1966, it was one of the longest single-span arches in the world. Traffic across this bridge was so heavy that a second bridge had to be built just a few miles downstream in 1996.

Although automobiles have largely replaced rail travel, trains are still a pleasant and efficient way to travel in Wales. Fast trains connect Welsh cities and towns to each other and the rest of Great Britain and there are links within the country. The Menai Suspension Bridge, designed by the great road builder Thomas Telford, connects the Isle of Anglesey with the mainland. Built in 1825, it has greatly improved the route between London and Holyhead.

The old Severn Bridge, one of the main routes into Wales.

The main international airport in Wales is in Cardiff, the entry point for international tourist flights. However, not all international airlines fly directly to Cardiff, and it is sometimes just as easy for international travelers to fly to London in England and then take the train to Cardiff, a journey of under two hours.

With such a long coastline, it is not surprising that Wales has many seaports. Ferries travel from Ireland to the ports of Holyhead, and the picturesque town of Fishguard. Other ports, such as Cardiff, Newport, Swansea, and Barry handle mainly cargo. The port at Milford Haven is one of the leading centers in western Europe that imports and refines oil.

THE WELSH

THERE IS SOMETHING UNIQUE about Wales. The people have distinctive accents, and in many areas of Wales, Welsh is spoken as a first language. But what really defines the Welsh is their spirit: passionate, down-to-earth, and warmhearted.

THE WELSH

The Welsh are descendents of the Celts, a fair-haired Aryan race who started migrating to Wales from mainland Europe from around 400 B.C. The Celts never established an empire, but by 300 B.C. their Iron Age culture prevailed throughout the British Isles. Invaders eventually pushed the Celts into the remote mountainous regions where they managed to maintain their unique culture. Many elements of Welsh culture evolved from the culture of the Celts.

Wales' small ethnic minority population can be found mainly in the cities of Cardiff, Swansea, and Newport.

Left: **Fair-haired Welsh girls.**

Opposite: **Welsh children in traditional costume.**

The Welsh delight in telling stories, and something as simple as travel directions is often embellished with history, folklore, and the latest local gossip. Their rich and powerful facility with words comes from the language itself, which is rooted in an ancient Celtic culture of myth and legend.

When the Welsh are not talking, they are probably singing. Music is close to the hearts of the people. Whether it is a casual singsong at the pub or a formal men's voice choir, the Welsh have a talent for singing. It is no wonder that Wales is often called the "Land of Song." The Welsh tradition of male voice choirs dates from the Industrial Revolution, when the overcrowding at Welsh industrial towns encouraged community events.

This men's voice choir is performing at the Welsh Folk Museum.

POPULATION

Only about 2.9 million people live in Wales, a mere 5% of the population of the United Kingdom. In fact, there are about twice as many sheep as there are people in Wales. For historical reasons, two-thirds of the population is concentrated in the south, in the cities of Cardiff, Swansea, and Newport, where the population is also more Anglicized than in the north. This is also one of the two industrial zones in Wales, the other being the coalfields in northeastern Wales.

As a once heavily industrialized region, South Wales attracted many immigrants in search of economic opportunities. From 1901–11, immigrants arrived here at a faster rate than any other country, with the exception of the United States. They came from other counties in Wales, from other parts of Great Britain, and European countries such as Italy and Poland.

BERTRAND RUSSELL (1872–1970): A FAMOUS WELSH PHILOSOPHER

Bertrand Russell is one of the most renowned logicians and philosophers of the 20th century. He was born in Trellick in Gwent, South Wales, but lived most of his life in England.

He published many books, having at one time more than 40 books in print, covering philosophy, mathematics, science, education, history, religion, and politics. His three-volumed *Principia Mathematica* (1910, 1912, and 1913) was immensely influential. In 1950 he won the Nobel Prize in Literature.

During World War I, his activities as a pacifist resulted in his being fined £100 in 1916, dismissed from his lectureship at Trinity College, and imprisoned for six months in 1918. In 1954 he made his famous "Man's Peril" broadcast on the British Broadcasting Corporation (BBC) condemning the Bikini H-bomb tests. He also set up an International War Crimes Tribunal to publicize alleged American atrocities in Vietnam. At the age of 83, Russell returned to Wales where he remained until his death.

THE WELSH IN AMERICA

In the 17th century groups of Welsh people went to America to escape persecution for their religious beliefs. Many of them made the state of Pennsylvania their home. Here they tried, unsuccessfully, to establish a Welsh utopia called Cambria, the ancient Roman name for Wales. Many people also went to America to look for economic opportunities. The Welsh coal miners and steelworkers who arrived in Pennsylvania in the 19th century helped to establish the coal and steel industries there.

People of Welsh extraction have distinguished themselves in America. John Llewellyn Lewis became the well-known leader of the United Mine Workers of America; and there have been four US presidents of Welsh extraction: Thomas Jefferson, James Monroe, Abraham Lincoln, and John Calvin Coolidge.

JOHN LLEWELLYN LEWIS (1880–1969)

Born in Iowa to immigrant parents from Welsh mining towns, John Llewellyn Lewis had to work in the coal mine from the age of 15. Starting as the head of a United Mine Workers of America (UMWA) local in 1911, he later became the president of UMWA from 1920 to 1960.

A giant among American leaders in the first half of the 20th century, Lewis was an adviser to presidents and a challenger to corporate leaders. A man of imposing appearance, with overhanging brows and a bulldog chin, Lewis was fond of using literary allusions and harsh epithets in his speeches. One of his speeches went: "I have pleaded your case from the pulpit and from the public platform—not in the quavering tones of a feeble mendicant asking alms, but in the thundering voice of the captain of a mighty host, demanding the rights to which free men are entitled."

Lewis helped to raise living standards for millions of Americans through his work in organizing industrial workers through the Congress of Industrial Organizations in the 1930s. He set up the UMWA Welfare and Retirement Fund, which improved healthcare for miners in the United States. President John Kennedy awarded Lewis the Presidential Medal of Freedom, the nation's highest civilian decoration, when he retired in 1960.

CLASS

Welsh society is not classless, but the social differences are not as obvious as in England. In England a person's accent is the most obvious sign of social class. When people talk about "BBC English," they are referring to the prestigious accent of the upper class. In England regional accents have traditionally been associated with the working class, although these days people of working-class origin might have middle-class jobs.

In Wales accents denote regional rather than social differences. You cannot determine whether you are speaking to a farmer or a managing director simply by the accent. The main reason for this is historical. When Wales was united with England (under the Acts of Union), members of the Welsh aristocracy moved to England and the landlords who stayed behind became Anglicized. They spoke English and felt closer to the English than to the majority of non-conformist Welsh-speakers. Hence the ordinary people were able to produce their own leaders, preachers, poets, and teachers and to establish their own social hierarchy.

ROBERT OWEN (1771–1858)

Robert Owen was a socialist held in high esteem by his countrymen. Born in Newton, Montgomeryshire, he left Wales to work in the cotton trade in Manchester. He worked his way up to the position of mill manager and became incredibly wealthy.

Owen was a kind employer who believed in social equality. He started the cooperative movement based on the premise that both consumers and workers would receive mutual benefits. He established an experimental workers' community in New Lanark, Scotland. In 1821 he set up a second model community in New Harmony, Indiana, in the United States. Here, he established the first free public library, kindergarten, and free public school.

He finally returned to Newton, where he died in 1858. The original furnishings from his home can now be seen in a memorial museum there.

LIFESTYLE

THE WELSH ARE A PATRIOTIC PEOPLE with a rich cultural heritage and a tradition of quality education at all levels. Proud of their national identity, they also enjoy strong community and family ties. Although the lifestyle in Wales is still mainly rural, it is becoming increasingly urbanized.

FAMILIES

In the old days, a family was a large collection of people that might live in the same town or village for generations. Grandmothers and grandfathers were very influential in a child's life and helped to reinforce values taught by the parents.

Today Welsh families are increasingly fragmented. Economic pressure has made it harder for families to all live in the same area, and grown-up

Left: **Families sunbathing next to Llyn Padarn in Llanberis.**

Opposite: **A joke shop in the popular seaside resort of Rhyl in North Wales.**

children often leave their hometown because they cannot find a suitable job there. Nevertheless, family ties are still important, and relatives get together on weekends or for special occasions.

A woman's traditional role in the family used to be that of a wife and mother. Nowadays it is considered acceptable for a wife and mother to be a career woman as well. In the last ten years, there has been a 17% increase in the employment rate for women with children between 5 and 10 years old. The increase in the number of working women has meant that couples tend to have fewer children—the average is 2.5 children—and tend to have their first child later in life, as late as age 30 to 34 years. There are also now more single mothers.

A young single mother with her baby and his grandmother.

HOUSING

Welsh houses are built in a variety of styles and from a range of materials. The Welsh like flowers and most homes have some sort of a garden, even if it is just a window box or a flower border. In the country there are quaint cottages built of stone and slate that were once mined in the local quarries. In cities such as Cardiff, there are semi-detached houses built of brick and modern materials.

Many cities and towns also have public or council houses that tenants can rent from the local council at a reasonable price. These were originally built for those who could not afford to buy a house, but today tenants have the option to buy their home from the council. There is a limited supply of public housing, so there are some who cannot afford to rent privately nor obtain council accommodation. Organizations such as Shelter give advice to the homeless and try to increase public awareness about this problem. Across Wales, the Welsh Office is responsible for the provision of new houses as well as the improvement of existing housing conditions.

Many Welsh houses are decked with flowers.

HEALTHCARE

The Welsh are getting healthier, and the life expectancy for men and women is 73 and 79 years respectively. Doctors are working hard to combat illnesses such as cancer and heart disease. Despite their efforts, respiratory diseases like bronchitis and emphysema still plague a number of former miners.

Up until the early part of the 20th century, people in some parts of Wales would consult the village "wise man" who used a number of different charms to cure diseases. Children with whooping coughs were supposed to make three visits to the wise man, and on each visit the child would eat a cake specially prepared to cure the ailment.

RURAL SETTLEMENT

Wales is predominately a rural country. There are a few towns and cities, but many picturesque villages are dotted across the countryside. The names of these villages, such as Llangybi in Gwynedd, North Wales, start with the prefix "Llan," meaning church. A typical Welsh village has a church surrounded by quaint cottages or small houses. There is usually a store, post office, and a pub where villagers can share a pint or two of beer. The pub is an institution in Wales where the locals can meet to exchange news and gossip.

Inevitably village life has changed. One of the consequences of rural depopulation was that English buyers snapped up empty country houses and farms as second homes. Of course this diluted local communities, but it also injected money and new skills into them. Nevertheless there was some hostility toward the influx of the English, and extremist groups such as the Sons of Glyndwr set over 130 second homes on fire during the late 1970s and throughout the 1980s.

Opposite: **A Welsh gynecologist and obstetrician.**

Today healthcare in Wales is provided through the National Health System (NHS). It is administered by local authorities and available to all people who register with a doctor near their home. Treatment is free, but there is a charge for prescriptions, although there are exemptions for the elderly. One of the most topical issues concerning the NHS is the waiting time for operations. NHS patients might have to wait a year or more if they need a non-urgent operation. In order to improve the level of service, the Patients Charter was launched in 1993 to set standards on how long people should wait for treatment. Despite this, some people still opt for private medical insurance plans with companies such as the British United Provident Association (BUPA).

In Great Britain working people contribute a portion of their salary toward the National Insurance Scheme. This money finances social benefits such as healthcare, unemployment benefits, and old age pensions. The government pension is low, and Great Britain's aging population puts additional pressure on the social security system. As a consequence, more people are making their own pension arrangements to ensure that they will have enough money to live on when they retire.

EDUCATION TODAY

Education is free and compulsory for Welsh children between the ages of 5 and 16. The Department for Education and Employment is responsible for the overall organization of education in England and Wales. The Welsh Assembly in Cardiff shares the responsibility of planning local educational syllabi with the Local Education Authorities (LEAs).

In the late 1980s, a National Curriculum—a set of national learning objectives—was introduced to raise the standard of education in Wales and throughout Great Britain. English, mathematics, and science are core subjects. In addition, in Welsh-speaking schools, Welsh is a core subject,

Below: **Children engaged in a competition at the Cardiff Science Park.**

Opposite: **The enrollment office of Menai College in Caernarfon, North Wales.**

but an elective subject in English-speaking schools. Other subjects include geography, history, music, art, technology, physical education, and information technology; and, in high school, or secondary school, a foreign language. The Welsh government aims to make the Welsh language compulsory in English-speaking schools by 2002. The number of pupils educated in the Welsh language is also increasing. In 1997 and 1998, about 30% of Welsh schoolchildren were educated entirely in Welsh. These Welsh-speaking schools are mainly found in the north and west of the country.

Children start elementary school at the age of four and enter secondary school when they are 11. Welsh children go to school from Monday to Friday, and the school day usually begins at 9 a.m. and finishes at 3:30 p.m. The children have about an hour for lunch, and they can either go home or eat

WELSH NOT

At one time there was prejudice against the Welsh language and a bias toward the use of English. The notorious "Welsh Not" plaque was a wooden sign with the words "Welsh Not" carved on it. This was hung around the neck of any pupil who was caught speaking Welsh. In 1847 an inflammatory report concerning the state of education was released that virulently attacked the standard of education in Wales and branded Welsh as the "language of slavery." It advised against using the Welsh language in schools and recommended more teaching in English. This outraged the Welsh and sparked a storm of controversy, which stimulated the drive for more schools, as well as free and compulsory education. It also fuelled the campaign for more Welsh in education. Today there are government grants to improve the standard of education in the Welsh language.

a sandwich at school. Parents can also pay for their child to have a hot lunch at school, and if they are poor, lunch will be provided free of charge.

The number of people enrolled in higher education is increasing. About 19% of men and 16% of women have a degree. Students can also receive Welsh-based education at colleges and at the University of Wales. Vocational education and training is also becoming more popular with young adults, and this is playing an important role in the economic regeneration of Wales.

IMPORTANT EDUCATIONAL INFLUENCES

Education has always been highly valued in Wales, although not widely available. Many working people of the past had little formal education but read voraciously to educate themselves.

A man who was very influential in the early days of education was Griffith Jones. His system of traveling preachers who taught people to read helped to make Wales literate. Another important figure, Thomas Charles (1755–1814), founded the Sunday Schools, which taught reading and writing and encouraged the discussion of theology. By the 19th century, two organizations, the British and Foreign Schools Society (established in 1808) and the National Society (established in 1811) started setting up more schools.

In 1870 the Education Act introduced a system of national elementary education, and school attendance was made compulsory by 1880. Local authorities set up "county schools" in 1889 to educate students up to the age of 18, and by 1902 places in these schools became free.

OWEN GLENDOWER (1354–1416)

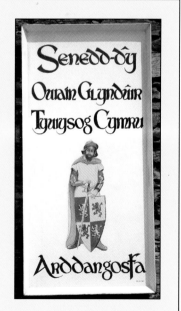

Owen Glendower is one of the greatest heroes in Welsh history. Born of noble Welsh lineage, he was a landowner who was educated in England. His noble birth gave Glendower credibility in the eyes of his countrymen, and he eventually led his people in a national revolt against the English. His bitter struggle began in 1400. By 1404 he had won control over most of Wales by forming alliances with King Henry IV's chief opponents.

Glendower managed to capture Harlech Castle and to form a parliament there and at Machynlleth. He had great plans for a Welsh nation, including the independence of the Welsh church from Canterbury and the creation of two Welsh universities. However, he did not live to implement many of his plans and his rebellion, the last major Welsh attempt to throw off English rule, eventually petered out. He was a hero to the Welsh nationalists in the 19th and 20th centuries.

RELIGION

THE MAJORITY OF WELSH ARE CHRISTIANS. The Christian religion has many denominations that differ in emphasis on the main tenets of Christianity. Some of the denominations found in Wales are the Church in Wales (Anglican), Presbyterian, Congregationalist, Roman Catholic, Baptist, Methodist, the Salvation Army, and the Society of Friends. Non-Christians are in the minority and are concentrated in the cities of Cardiff, Newport, and Swansea. These include Buddhists, Hindus, Jews, Sikhs, and Muslims.

THE AGE OF SAINTS

After the Romans left, Wales entered a period marked by frequent wars and a disintegration of urban life. These times have been referred to both as the Dark Ages and the Age of Saints. Although the Romans had planted

Left: **St. David's Cathedral, named after its patron saint, dates from the 12th century.**

Opposite: **The bedroom in a Welsh miner's cottage has a reminder that God is never far away.**

the seeds of Christianity, it was not until traveling Christian missionaries began spreading the faith in the fifth century that the majority of the population converted. These missionaries were called *sancti,* meaning saints, and were influential in Wales. They built monasteries, hospices, and churches and were said to have miraculous healing powers. Saint David, who lived in South Wales in the sixth century, became the patron saint of Wales.

CHRISTIANITY

The majority of Welsh people are Christians. The Christian church has three main denominations—Protestant, Roman Catholic, and Orthodox. Although church services vary among them, they share certain common beliefs. All Christians believe there is only one God, and that he is the creator and ruler of the universe. They believe that Jesus was the Son of God and the saviour of mankind, and that the Bible is inspired by God. The Bible is divided into the Old Testament and the New Testament.

SAINT DAVID (A.D. 520–600)

Saint David (Dewi in Welsh) is the patron saint of Wales. He was born near St. Bride's Bay, Pembrokeshire, and his mother was a holy woman called Saint Non. Following his education he set up numerous churches throughout South Wales. More than 50 churches have been named after him and still exist today. He moved the seat of ecclesiastical (church) government from Caerleon to Mynyw, which is still the cathedral city of western Wales today. Saint David set up a religious community there that emphasized a frugal lifestyle. Although he lived on bread, herbs, and water, he was reputed to be 6 feet (2 m) tall, handsome, and very strong. He died in A.D. 600, and his last words were, "Be cheerful and keep your faith." The Cathedral of St. David's, where he is buried, is now a place of pilgrimage, and his feast day is on March 1.

The Old Testament is a history of the Jewish people and contains the prophecy that a Messiah will come to earth in preparation for the kingdom of God. Christians believe that Jesus is this Messiah. The New Testament was written by Jesus' followers and tells about his life and teaching.

THE ANGLICAN CHURCH

There are about 108,000 members of the Anglican Church in Wales. Anglicans reject the authority of the Pope and other aspects of Roman Catholicism. The organization of the Anglican Church is rather hierarchical. Its clergy are called vicars, and the senior clergy members are called bishops. The Church in Wales originated from the Church of England, which used to be the official Welsh state church. In 1920 the Church in Wales severed its ties with the Church of England and was no longer subject to parliament.

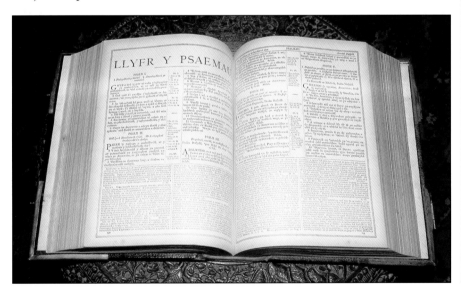

A Welsh Bible dating from 1880. Bishop Morgan's Welsh translation in 1588 greatly influenced the spread of the Welsh language.

ROMAN CATHOLIC CHURCH

There are 60,000 Roman Catholics in Wales, a small but rapidly growing minority, mainly in the northeast. Roman Catholics consider the Pope the spiritual head of the church and any decisions he makes concerning matters of the faith are binding on all Catholics. The current pope is John Paul II, who lives in the Vatican City, an independant state in Rome, Italy, and the spiritual center of the Roman Catholic church.

Roman Catholics believe that only through the priest can God forgive men for their sins, so they make regular visits to Confession, where they confess their sins to the priest and ask for God's forgiveness. All Christians believe in life after death, but only Catholics believe in purgatory, a state

Roman Catholics lining up to receive Holy Communion.

between heaven and hell that is a temporary place of purification. Roman Catholics pray to Mary, the mother of Jesus, and most churches have a picture or statue of her. Catholics use rosary beads when they say a special prayer to Mary. The Catholic Church also recognizes many saints.

The Holy Communion service, known as Mass to the Catholics, is one of the most important ceremonies in all Christian churches. It remembers events at Jesus' Last Supper. When Jesus was eating with his disciples, he took some bread, gave thanks, broke it, and gave it to his disciples, saying, "Take and eat; this is my body." Then he took the cup, gave thanks, and offered it to them, saying, "Drink from it, all of you. This is my blood of the covenant, which is poured out for many for the forgiveness of sins." Roman Catholics believe that the bread and wine given by the priest as part of the service really become Christ's body and blood, while most Protestants believe that they represent Christ's body and blood on the cross, on which he died to take God's punishment for all people's sins. In Roman Catholic churches, Holy Communion is received at the altar and can be celebrated daily. Other denominations celebrate it only a few times a month and on special occasions such as Christmas.

MONASTERIES

Wales has many monasteries. In the early days of Christianity, many missionaries traveled along the western coast, and some settled on Caldey Island. The Benedictines established an order there in the 12th century and stayed until the dissolution of the monasteries by Henry VIII in 1536 and 1539. Today Caldey Island has a community of monks (of the Cistercian Order) who work the land and make perfume from gorse and lavender. This community is virtually secluded from the world. Its monks keep a harsh routine and practise ceaseless devotions. Barely 3 miles (5 km) from one of Wales' most popular seaside resorts, it supports itself by selling its famous perfume in gift shops and by mail order.

The pretty gardens of St. John's Methodist church in Colwyn Bay.

FREE CHURCHES AND NON-CONFORMISTS

Wales has a history of non-conformity in religion. Although once the official state church in Wales, the Church of England had fallen out of favor with many Welsh people by the 19th century. There were many reasons for this. One of the most decisive was that the Church of England was seen to be pro-English, politically Conservative, and like the Welsh landowners, remote from the ordinary people. As a result, many working people broke away from the established church and joined non-conformist groups. By 1851, 80% of the population was non-conformist. The largest non-conformist group, particularly in the rural areas, was the Calvinist Methodists. Other popular groups were the Congregationalists (or Independents), Baptists, Wesleyans, and groups like the Salvation Army.

Methodism was introduced to Wales in the mid-18th century in a form similar to Calvinism. Two of the most famous Welsh Methodist preachers were David Rowlands and Howell Harris. The Calvinistic Methodists are now a branch of the Presbyterian church.

Today non-conformists are usually called members of free churches. Like the Anglicans, they reject the infallibility of the Pope and the right of a priest to forgive sins. However, non-conformists put less emphasis on liturgy than the Anglican Church and their services are less formal. There are about 220,300 members of non-conformist groups in Wales today.

CHAPELS

Although they are small and spartan, Welsh chapels have a simple beauty of their own. More importantly, they stand as a symbol of the nation's religious revival in the 18th century and a reminder of a way of life that has now passed.

In the second half of the 19th century, chapels sprang up all over Wales. So great was the building boom that it was estimated that a new chapel was built every eight days. Chapels and their ministers greatly influenced community life and became involved in politics. Great choirs and bands were born under their roofs, and their Sunday Schools played an important role in Welsh education and the survival of the Welsh language.

In the 1860s the chapels advocated the "Temperance Movement," which frowned upon alcohol, pubs, and opening shops on Sundays. As a result, fewer Welsh attended chapel services, as they found the preaching too restrictive. By the early 1900s the chapels began losing followers, and by the beginning of this century, the influence of non-conformist chapels has declined.

The Society of Friends (Quakers) gather in their own meeting houses rather than in churches. They do not have priests because they believe God speaks directly to all believers. During a Quaker service, people usually sit in a circle, and nobody utters a word as every member quietly thinks of God.

73

LANGUAGE

IF YOU ARE DRIVING THROUGH Wales, you will see that the road signs and place names appear in both English and Welsh. Everybody in Wales speaks English and about one-fifth of the population also speak Welsh, an ancient language rooted in Celtic culture.

THE WELSH LANGUAGE

Welsh is the oldest living language in Great Britain and is one of six Celtic languages belonging to the Indo-European family of languages. It evolved from the language of the ancient Brythons. Although written Welsh is the standard, there are different regional accents and dialect variations.

About 20% of the population speak Welsh. In the north and west, more than 80% of the population speak the language, whereas Welsh speakers

In 1995–96 the Welsh Office provided about 6.3 million pounds in grants to promote the Welsh language.

Left: **Road signs in Wales are usually in both English and Welsh.**

Opposite: **A woman in front of a bookshop in Hay-on-Wye, known in Wales as the "Town of Books."**

The Welsh language is closer to Breton, which is spoken in Brittany, France, than it is to the Gaelic languages of Ireland and Scotland.

in the south and east number as few as below 10%. The language has been threatened by an ever-increasing exposure to the English language, the most significant being during the Industrial Revolution when there was a great influx of English to work in the Welsh mines. By 1901 English speakers outnumbered Welsh speakers for the first time.

Yet, it seems that the Welsh language is destined to survive. Between 1989 and 1995, the number of pupils in elementary classes where Welsh was the main language of instruction increased by 36%, and there has been a renewed interest in the language, particularly in the Anglicized areas of South Wales. It is now also possible to be educated in Welsh from elementary school through to university.

Teenagers chatting on a street in Bangor in North Wales.

THE CAMPAIGN TO SAVE THE LANGUAGE

Since the 1960s, both the government and Welsh language enthusiasts have tried to maintain the language and to give it an official status. In 1962 Saunders Lewis, one of the founders of the Plaid Cymru party, delivered a powerful lecture concerning the "fate of the language." This fuelled public concern about the language, and a few months later the Welsh Language Society was founded. It began a series of successful campaigns in the pursuit of bilingualism, and today it is unusual to see road and town signs that are not in both English and Welsh.

Legislation in favor of the Welsh language has also been introduced. In 1967 the Welsh Language Act gave Welsh speakers the right to use the Welsh language in court. Demands for more legislation to support the rights of Welsh speakers led to a new Language Act (1993), which gave the language equal status in the public sector. A Welsh Language Board was also established to promote the use of the language. Nowadays, most information in Wales (such as telephone bills and tax forms) is bilingual.

Samples of the Welsh newspaper *Y Cymro*, which means "The Welshman."

MEDIA

The growth in Welsh-language media has injected new life into the language. Prior to 1982, Welsh-language television programs were only broadcast for a few hours on BBC and ITV (Independent Television). The government finally yielded to Welsh demands, and S4C (*Sianel Pedwar Cymru* or Channel Four Wales) began broadcasting in 1982, stimulating the Welsh film and television industry. Cardiff is now one of the most active television production centers in Britain, especially in the area of animation. In addition, Radio Cymru transmits in Welsh.

Wales has both English and Welsh newspapers. Britain's national newspapers like *The Independent* and *The Guardian* provide news about Britain and the world. The closest Wales has to a national newspaper is *The Western Mail*, which is written in English. There are plans to launch a daily Welsh-language newspaper on the World Wide Web. There are also many local newspapers and magazines that are published entirely in the Welsh language such as *Y Cymro*, a weekly newspaper.

SPEAKING WELSH

The Welsh language may be daunting to a stranger. It is amazing that anyone can get their tongue around the name of a tiny village in Anglesey: *Llanfairpwllgwyngyllgogerychwyrndrobwllllantysiliogogogoch*—possibly the longest word in the world! This name means "Church of St. Mary in the Hollow by the White Aspen near the Rapid Whirlpool and Church of St. Tysilio by the Red Cave."

Many place names, such as Llangollen, begin with the prefix *Llan*, which means "church." The double "l" is a little difficult to say because there is no English equivalent. If you want to try to say it, put your tongue behind your teeth and blow out to make a sound like "thlan."

The Welsh language is also full of imaginative first names. Girls have pretty names like Bronwen, Megan, and Ceri. Boys have names like Dylan, Aneurin, and Dafydd. There are fewer surnames, so the names Morgan, Jones, Evans, Williams, and Lloyd are quite common. Some surnames contain the prefix "AP," which means "son of." So the name "AP Owen" means "son of Owen."

The Welsh town with the longest name in the world.

A BIBLIOPHILE'S DREAM

The number of books printed in Welsh flourished after printing was introduced to Wales in 1718. Today publishers like Gomer Press, Y Lolfa, and the University of Wales encourage Welsh writers. The Welsh Books Council was set up in 1961 to encourage Welsh-language publishing. It provides grants to Welsh-language publishers and runs a children's book club.

The small town of Hay-on-Wye has a reputation as the secondhand book capital of Wales, and it holds a Festival of Literature every summer. There are bookshops everywhere selling books on all sorts of unusual subjects ranging from general interest to the occult. The town evolved from a market town to a town of books in the 1960s, when Richard Booth set up a book and antiques store. The demand for old books was so great that Booth began snapping up property to set up other bookstores. Even an old castle began selling books! Booth was a colorful character in his own right, and at one stage he declared Hay-on-Wye an independent state, issuing its own passports and currency.

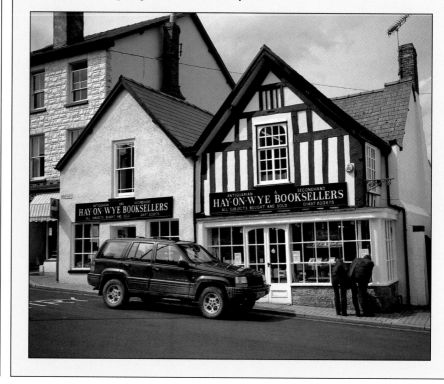

LETTERS AND SOUNDS

Welsh may not be the easiest language to master, but it helps to know how to pronounce the letters. The Welsh alphabet is similar to the English one with a few differences. There are seven vowels ("a-e-i-o-u-w-y") instead of five. Most of the vowels, except "y," have a short and a long sound. For example the "a" in *tad* (which means father) is long as in the word hard, and in the word *mam* (which means mother) it is short as in ham. The language also has lots of adjoining vowels (such as "ae," "ai," "oe"), and both vowels are pronounced, but the stress is usually on the first.

The Welsh language does not have the consonants "j," "k," "v," "x," and "z," but there are some additional ones: "ch," "dd," "ff," "ll," "ph," and "th." In Welsh, "c" is always hard, so *Cymru* (the Welsh word for Wales) is pronounced as "COME-ri." The letter "w" is pronounced as "oo." So the word *drws* (which means door) is pronounced as "DROOS." The letter "f" is always pronounced like "v" and the letter "g" is always hard, as in "get." The letters "dd" sound like the letters "th" in "them," so *yn dda* (which means good) sounds like "UN thah."

Many towns and villages have English and a Welsh name: Cardiff or Caerdydd; Swansea or Abertawe; and Brecon or Aberhonddu are just a few examples.

A FEW WELSH WORDS AND PHRASES

Good morning—*Bore da* ("BORREH-dah")
Good afternoon—*P'nawn da* ("PN-own-dah")
How are you?—*Sut mae?* ("SIT-my")
Welcome—*Croeso* ("CROY-so")
Please—*Os gwelwch yn dda* ("OS-goo-ell-w-ch-un-thah")
Thank you—*Diolch* ("DEE-ol-ch")
Goodbye—*Hwyl* ("HOO-eel")

ARTS

MUSIC AND POETRY ARE ALIVE in the hearts of the Welsh people. This lyrical land has plenty of vibrant men's choirs, sweet-sounding singers, gentle harpists, and imaginative poets. Beyond poetry and music, there are other treasures: grey stone castles, theatrical performers, and a long-standing tradition of craft.

LITERATURE

Wales is a land of myths and legends—of fire-breathing dragons, mysterious wizards and forbidding giants. Many legends spring from the *Mabinogion,* a great medieval collection of Celtic folktales.

Beyond magical tales, there is a substantial body of contemporary writing, and many Welsh writers have been published by both English

Left: **The crowning of the bard at the National Eisteddfod. The arch-druid (a former bard himself) places the crown on the winner's head.**

Opposite: **A lovespoon and stick carver proudly displays his work.**

One of the oldest surviving Welsh poems, Y Gododdin, *tells the story of a battle in Yorkshire (in modern day England). It was composed by a poet known as Aneirin around* A.D. *600.*

and Welsh companies. Distinguished 20th century writers include Richard Llewellyn, famous for his work *How Green Was My Valley?*, Kate Roberts, Sir Thomas Parry-Williams, Saunders Lewis, and R. Williams Parry.

POETRY

The Welsh have always had a flair for poetry. Long ago great kings like Hywel the Great paid poets to perform. Known as bards, they told magical tales and composed eulogies and elegies for princes and noblemen. Taliesin was a famous sixth-century poet who wrote poems in praise of a king named Urien of Rheged.

The bards were elite members of society and each prince had his own court poet who earned his position through competition at a festival called the *eisteddfod* ("ACE-deth-vord"). During an *eisteddfod* (singular), contests in poetry, music, and literature are held. Modern poets still compete against each other at the hundreds of *eisteddfodau* ("ACE-deth-vord-eye") that are held in villages and towns throughout Wales. The biggest is the Royal National Eisteddfod, which is held every year in Wales.

Wales has continued to produce outstanding poets. Alun Lewis (1915–44) caught the public's attention with his poems about the grim conditions in the army camps during World War II. Most of his poems in *Raider's Dawn* (1942) and short stories in *The Last Inspection* (1942) are about army life in training camps in England. His most famous poem is *All Day It Has Rained*. Another poet of distinction is William Henry Davies (1871–1940). Born in Newport, Davies started out as an apprentice to a picture framer, but lived the life of a wanderer, tramping through the United States, losing a foot while trying to jump a train in Canada and becoming a peddler and street singer in England. His *Autobiography of a Super-*

Tramp (1907) appeared with a preface by George Bernard Shaw. He received wide popularity for this and other works, such as *The Loneliest Mountain* (1939). Ronald Stuart Thomas, born in Cardiff in 1913, writes poetry with a strong cultural and moral consciousness. However, the most renowned Welsh poet is undoubtedly Dylan Thomas.

DYLAN THOMAS (1914–53)

Dylan Thomas was born in Swansea in 1914. His father, who was an English teacher, introduced him to literature at a young age. Young Thomas began his career as a newspaper reporter in Swansea. His thirst for adventure took him to London where he immersed himself in the literary scene. He was a colorful and popular character in the clubs where he spent many a night conversing with his cronies.

Although Dylan came from a Welsh-speaking family, he did not speak any Welsh, which irked some of his fellow Welshmen. Although he was often misunderstood, it is clear from his work that he had a great affection for his country. His poems and stories are distinctively Welsh in their rhythmic quality and draw on his childhood in Wales. His well-known *Under Milk Wood* is a popular radio play that delves into the thoughts and lives of a small Welsh seaside community.

His *Collection of Poems* distinguished him as one of the great English-speaking poets of modern times. Dylan's most famous lines are those he wrote for his dying father: "Do not go gentle into that good night/Rage, rage against the dying of light." Dylan himself died at the young age of 39 from an overdose of hard liquor.

MUSIC

The Welsh have a passion for music. For so small a country, there is an incredible reservoir of talent, from opera singers such as the late Sir Geraint Evans, Bryn Terfel, and Dame Margaret Price to pop stars like Tom Jones and Shirley Bassey.

During the 1970s, South Wales rock bands became popular, and in the 1980s protest singers such as Meic Stephens came onto the scene. Many Welsh rock bands have influenced the campaign to protect the language, and bilingual bands such as Catatonia are enjoying international success.

The Welsh have a gift for singing and are world-renowned for their men's choirs. Choirs have always been a strong part of popular culture in the valleys. This choral tradition dates back to the 19th century and is still carried on by great choirs such as the Pendyrus.

Shirley Bassey singing with the World Choir and the Royal Philharmonic Orchestra.

HYMNS

The Welsh are especially fond of singing hymns, a tradition that goes back to the days of the Methodist chapels. Their favorites are *Cym Rhondda* and *Land of our Fathers* (the national anthem). You will hear them sung in schools, at political meetings, rugby matches, and just about any place where there is a crowd.

William Williams (1717–91), also called Williams Pantycelyn, was the leader of the Methodist revival in Wales and its chief hymn writer. He wrote some 800 hymns, including *Guide me, O Thou Great Jehovah*. Although William Williams had a wider public audience, Ann Griffiths (1776–1805) also composed beautiful hymns, which she wrote down on bits of paper and shared with visiting preachers who came to her house.

A harpist performing at the National Eisteddfod.

FOLK MUSIC AND INSTRUMENTS

Welsh folk music is dear to the Welsh. One of the most popular songwriters is Dafydd Iwan who uses music to convey political messages. Another well-known musician in Wales is Tudor Morgan. He has worked on collaborations to produce song and music based on the *Mabinogian*.

Folk musicians use a number of instruments, but for centuries the harp has been the most important among them. In the 19th century the Welsh triple harp (with three rows of strings) superceded the simple harp. Although once thought to have been invented in Wales, the triple harp was in fact one of the Italian Baroque instruments invented one hundred years earlier.

During the 19th century, there was a trend toward classical concert music, which introduced the large, chromatic pedal harp to Welsh music. But the gypsy musicians kept playing the triple harp because it was lighter for them to carry around. Today the triple harp is regarded as the national instrument of Wales. It is used in conjunction with folk singing or as a solo instrument. The most influential triple harpist today is Robin Huw Bowen, who has performed throughout Europe and North America.

The towering Caernarfon Castle, a crusader-style castle and one of the many majestic castles built by King Edward I.

ARCHITECTURE

Welsh buildings tend to be simpler than those in England because after the union in 1536, the Welsh aristocrats moved to London, taking the most talented architects and artists with them. Although Wales is not an architectural gem, it does have more castles per square mile than any other country in Europe. There are hundreds of them ranging from Roman fortresses to Norman and Saxon forts. Some of the most impressive are those built by King Edward I.

Beaumaris Castle is an ingenious fortress that was built on the Isle of Anglesey to protect shipping in the Menai Strait. Caernarfon Castle in North Wales is probably the most striking medieval castle in Wales. Its sheer scale and commanding presence are testimony to King Edward's intention for it to be a symbol of English dominance. Its colorful stonework and octagonal towers were modeled on Byzantine castles. In 1969 the castle became internationally famous when Prince Charles was invested there as Prince of Wales.

THE ITALIAN VILLAGE

One of the most intriguing sites in Cardigan Bay, North Wales, is an Italian-style village called Portmeirion, conceived by Sir Clough William-Ellis (1883–1978). It was a fulfillment of his childhood dream to build a village "of my own fancy on chosen site."

The village was built gradually over the years from 1925 to 1972 and combines color-washed buildings, statues, and fountains with a variety of architectural styles including Georgian, Victorian, Oriental, and Gothic. There are about 50 buildings centered on a piazza. This includes the luxurious Portmeirion Hotel, which boasts furniture from Rajasthan, India; quaint village cottages; and a shop selling flowered pottery. Portmerion had been the location for several films and television programs, including the 1960s television series *The Prisoner*.

FOLLY CASTLES

Some of Wales' most impressive castles are less than 150 years old. These so-called "folly" castles were built during the 19th century to display the wealth of the nouveau riche, the coal barons and business tycoons who profited from the industrial boom. One of these is Castle Coch, situated just outside Cardiff.

This fairytale castle is a reconstruction of a 13th century castle, complete with a drawbridge and murder holes. The interior is a Victorian fantasy with lavish murals, mirrored ceilings, and walls decorated with scenes from Aesop's fables. It was created by the architect William Burges for his wealthy patron, the Marquess of Bute.

ARTS AND CRAFTS

Wales is a flourishing center for crafts, and Welsh craftsmen have always had an eye for making useful items beautiful. Their Celtic ancestors also had an appreciation of beautiful things, and their art was rather abstract. They liked to use swirling and round shapes, which modern craftsmen have preserved in their pottery, jewelry, woodcarving, and sculpture.

With so many sheep, it is no surprise that Wales has a longstanding tradition of craft in wool. Spinning, weaving, and knitting date back to the days when merchants used to take Welsh stockings and socks to the markets of London. Today you can still find cozy, hand-knitted sweaters, woven blankets, and tapestry quilts with skillful embroidery.

Clay figure maker at work.

The Welsh landscape has inspired both native and immigrant painters. Although he is known as the father of British landscape painting, Richard Wilson spent most of his life in London and Italy, and his paintings were mainly of Welsh subjects. Among Wales' most famous painters are Sir Frank Brangwyn, Cedric Morris, Augustus John and his sister Gwen John, Ceri Richards, and Kyffin Williams.

FILM AND THEATER

Many famous actors and actresses are Welsh, including Richard Burton, Sir Anthony Hopkins, and Catherine Zeta-Jones. The latest Welsh heartthrob is 25-year-old Ioan Gruffydd, a Welsh-language soap star who became an overnight sensation after his role as the officer who saved Kate Winslet in the film *Titanic*.

WELSH LOVESPOONS

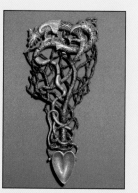

Until the 19th century, it was a Welsh custom for a young man to carve a wooden spoon and give it to his sweetheart as an indication of his intention to marry her. Once received, the spoons were often hung on the wall as a reminder of the suitor.

The spoon itself was a symbol that the suitor would take care of his loved one. The designs of the spoons had various meanings, and the maker would choose his own personal symbols. Hearts were popular motifs, and a double heart meant the young man and his girl were united. Miniature houses represented building a home together.

Nowadays lovespoons have taken on a wider meaning. They are carved to commemorate events other than marriage and are given as gifts on occasions such as birthdays. Most lovespoons today are mass-produced, but those who are sentimental can commission a craftsman to personalize their spoons.

Although the center of British theater is in London, Wales has its own theater companies that produce their own plays and invite visiting companies. There is a small film culture in Wales, but financial constraints have forced the best talent to look for opportunities elsewhere. Filmmaker Chris Monger returned to South Wales in 1994 to make a well-known film about Wales—*The Englishman who Went up a Hill and Came Down a Mountain*, starring Hugh Grant. The Welsh director Endaf Emlyn was nominated for a Hollywood Academy Award in 1994 for *Hedd Wynn*, a film about a poet killed in World War I.

ANTHONY HOPKINS (1937–)

Born in 1937 in Port Talbot, South Wales, Philip Anthony Hopkins was the only child of a baker. He joined a community junior drama club at 17, attended the Welsh College of Music and Drama in Cardiff, and went on to win a scholarship to the prestigious Royal Academy of Dramatic Art in London in 1961. Obtaining a place with the National Theater after an audition with his idol, Laurence Olivier, Hopkins went on to enjoy immense stage success at the Old Vic theater.

His first film role was in the 1968 in *The Lion in Winter*, starring as Richard the Lionheart opposite Peter O'Toole and Katharine Hepburn. Since then, he has appeared in some 90 movies. His portrayal of Hannibal Lecter in *The Silence of the Lambs*, depicting an uncanny intelligence and startling tenderness behind sadistic malice, made him the darling of American audiences. With an Academy Award for Best Actor in his pocket for that performance, he went on to star in the 1992 Merchant-Ivory *Howard's End*, and the 1993 *Remains of the Day*. His latest films are *Meet Joe Black*, *Legends of the Fall*, and *The Mask of Zorro*.

He received the title of Commander, Order of the British Empire, from Queen Elizabeth in 1987; and became an American citizen in 2000.

LEISURE

LEISURE PLAYS AN IMPORTANT PART in the lives of most Welsh people. For many, sports are the main form of entertainment. The Welsh are particularly passionate about rugby, but they also enjoy soccer, cricket, and outdoor games.

RUGBY

The sport that really excites the Welsh is rugby. Rugby is a ball game that is similar (but not the same) to American football: players try to carry an egg-shaped ball over the opposing team's line, and there are huddles, called scrums. Rugby fans are devoted and matches draw huge crowds of fans clad in red scarves and hats, waving the Welsh flag and carrying leeks.

In 1999 Wales hosted the Rugby World Cup, which is the world's third largest televised event after the soccer World Cup. One of Wales' biggest games is the International, which takes place twice a year in winter. This is the match where Wales plays England and Ireland one year, and France and Scotland the next. Another competition is the Triple Crown, which is awarded to the nation that beats the other three nations of Britain.

Rugby has come to be regarded as the national game of Wales, and many of the players have become legends. An outstanding example is Teddy Morgan, whose performance during the 1905 International match against New Zealand will never be forgotten. The New Zealand team had won all 26 games on their tour, until this small Welsh man scored the only try and won the match for Wales.

Above: **Gregor Townsend in the 1998 Wales vs Scotland rugby match.**

Opposite: **Sailing on Llangorse Lake in Mid-Wales.**

OTHER POPULAR SPORTS

Other popular sports in Wales include football, cricket, and baseball. Both men and women play football (or soccer as it is called in the United States), but fewer women and children go to football matches than men. Cricket is played throughout Wales, and the main team is Glamorgan, which competes with some of the best teams in England. Baseball, an American import, is particularly popular in southeastern Wales. One of the newest spectator sports in Wales is ice hockey, played at the National Ice Rink in Cardiff. Wales also has over a hundred golf courses. The two best known are Royal St. David's in Mid-Wales, which is overlooked by Harlech Castle, and Royal Porthcawl, a 107-year-old course in South Wales.

Rugby fans outside the Millennium Stadium after the Wales vs Argentina match on October 1, 1999.

CLUBS

Welsh people attach great importance to personal contacts; therefore pubs, clubs, and activity centers play an important part in their lives. In these places they can meet others who share similar interests.

The YMCA, the Scouts, Girl Guides, and church groups are all active in Wales. The Youth Service in Wales is an organization that aims to develop social and cultural education for young people. Wales is also one of Britain's largest centers for gymnastics with over 60 clubs.

Multi-sports and leisure centers sprung up in the 1970s and 1980s to cater to the health and fitness craze. The David Lloyd George Sports Center in Cardiff has aerobics classes, a big swimming pool, and a weight training room.

The Wales vs Brazil soccer match on May 23, 2000.

WELSH TALENT

There is no shortage of talented sports people in Wales. From 1994 to 1995, Wales had 131 performers who became British champions. Colin Jackson won a gold medal in the 361-feet (110-m) hurdles at the 1993 World Championships in Germany and a silver medal at the 1998 Olympics. Wales also has a national team that competes in the Commonwealth games; and in 1994 Welsh athletes won 19 medals.

One of the most successful disabled female athletes is Tanni Grey, who set a world record in 1996 in the Elite Ladies' Wheelchair marathon in London. She won four gold medals and broke three world records at the 1992 paralympics in Barcelona, and won another four gold medals in the 1995 World Championships.

The Sports Council is a government-financed agency that strives to increase participation in sport and to elevate the standards of performance. It provides grants and services to clubs for training and competition. The most talented sportsmen and women receive assistance through a program known as Elite Cymru.

BACK TO NATURE

The Welsh are great nature lovers and have a deep respect for the countryside. National parks were set up in the 1950s to conserve Areas of Outstanding Natural Beauty. Wales has three national parks—Snowdonia, Pembrokeshire Coast, and the Brecon Beacons. These offer activities such as hiking, farm holidays, pony trekking, climbing, and canoeing. There are also nature trails and country parks such as the Forest Center in Brecon Beacons, and the National Water Sports Center at Caernarfon. At the foot of Mount Snowdon, the villages of Beddgelert, Betws-y-Coed, and Llanberis are popular bases for walkers.

Children canoeing on Llangorse Lake in Mid-Wales.

Hikers enjoying the view at the Brecon Beacons.

BRECON BEACONS NATIONAL PARK

The Brecon Beacons National Park is a mixture of varied terrain and mountains: in the east lie the Black Mountains; in the west the remote Black Mountain; and the Beacons themselves, with Pen-y-Fan, stand at 2,908 feet (886 m), the highest point in South Wales. The southern mountains are more challenging than they look, and inexperienced walkers often overestimate how far they can walk. The grass is knee-high in parts, which can slow down walkers, and the mountains look similar, so unless one is a good map-reader, it is easy to get lost. The weather there is volatile and harsh. There can be intense rain, heavy mist, and biting winds; not to mention the temperature drops about 41°F (5°C) for every 3,282 feet (1,000 m) climbed. The Ystrad Falls in the west of the park are even more dangerous. Here ravines, gorges, and fast-falling waters have caused many accidents. That said, for those who are careful, a walk in the park can be a safe yet exhilarating experience.

VACATIONS

Many Welsh like to escape to the seaside. This has been a popular destination for more than 100 years when seaside resort towns sprang up to cater to tourists. One of the largest resorts in Wales is Llandudno, where Victorian houses line the shores like those on a picture postcard. Farther south at Portcawl, camp grounds are dotted along the coast. Here, children can enjoy donkey rides and other amusements.

Another traditional vacation destination is vacation camp, where accommodation, meals, and entertainment are organized for visitors. These were very popular in the 1950s and 1960s, and Butlin's and Pontin's, the companies that arranged them, are well-known names. This tradition has declined slightly in popularity over the past 30 years as more Welsh vacation abroad.

Above: **A man who has just been rescued from the turbulent waters of the Severn estuary in a Sea King rescue helicopter.**

Left: **Vacationers crowd the beach at Llandudno.**

FESTIVALS

THE WELSH ENJOY THE SAME HOLIDAYS as the rest of Great Britain, but they also have their own festivals to celebrate their unique culture and language. There are music, art, poetry, and even agricultural festivals throughout Wales. Some of these events, such as the Royal National Eisteddfod, are such grand-scale events that they draw a large international audience every year.

THE ROYAL NATIONAL EISTEDDFOD

The Royal National Eisteddfod is the great cultural event in Wales, and it takes place solely in the Welsh language. An *eisteddfod* is simply a public meeting where contests in poetry, music, and literature are held. Hundreds of them are held throughout the year in Wales, but the Royal National Eisteddfod is world renowned. It dates back 100 years and has grown

Left: **Singers from Brazil participating in the Llangollen International Eisteddfod, a seven-day extravaganza of music and dance started in Wales in 1947.**

Opposite: **Merrymakers dressed in Victorian costume and street entertainers participating in a street parade.**

103

The Proclamation Ceremony at the Logan Stone, conducted by the Archdruid, is when the date for the next year's National Eisteddfod is announced.

to include everything from poetry and dancing to rock bands. Every competitor dreams of competing at the Royal National Eisteddfod, perhaps to win the crown or the bardic chair, two of the most prestigious prizes for the best poems. The custom of awarding a chair rather than a trophy goes back to the time when the court poets of a particular king or prince won an official seat, or chair, in the royal household.

The Gorsedd ("GOR-seth") of Bards awards these coveted prizes with great pomp and ceremony. The Gorsedd is an association of people with an interest in Welsh literature and music. It was established by an eccentric scholar named Edward Williams (or Iolo Morganwg in Welsh) in 1792. He believed that an ancient order of druids had survived in Wales and that he was a descendent of that ancient order. Although they have nothing to do with druids, members of the Gorsedd of Bards are still known as druids and wear different colored robes to signify their rank.

In addition to the Royal National Eisteddfod, there is the International Musical Festival, held every July in the small town of Llangollen in North

Wales. Performers from over 40 countries come here to sing, dance, and play their musical instruments. An interesting feature of this event is that overseas visitors stay at the homes of the local people free of charge. The Urdd National Eisteddfod is a festival for people under 25 that takes place in May.

The largest arts festival in Wales is the Swansea Festival of Music and Arts, held in September, which includes theater, opera, dance, jazz, and literary events. Equally important is the Brecon Jazz Festival in August, a three-day festival held in the tranquil town of Brecon.

Schoolchildren performing the floral dance in front of the Gorsedd of Bards of the Isle Britain. The Maid of Honor, attended by two page boys, is seen holding the Horn of Plenty.

ST. DAVID'S DAY

Every year on March 1, the Welsh celebrate St. David's Day, and many people wear leeks on this day. Born in the sixth century A.D., Saint David studied for the priesthood, was called to missionary life, and founded numerous monasteries. His burial place, at St. David's Cathedral in the town of St. David, is now a center of pilgrimage.

There are many legends about the patron saint of Wales. It is said that when he and his monks first arrived in Glyn Rhosyn, a local chief named Boia was terrorizing the area. To drive out the monks, Boia's wife tried to tempt them to break their vows by sending her maids naked to the monastery. Determined to set a good example, St. David promptly sent the girls home. It is also said that when St. David died a host of singing angels took him to heaven.

WELSH FOLK COSTUME

On St. David's Day, and on other special occasions, you may see Welsh women and children wearing colorful costumes with tall black hats and red cloaks. This is the Welsh national costume, and it developed from the clothing that countrywomen wore in the 19th century, namely a flannel bathrobe worn as a coat over a striped flannel petticoat with an apron, shawl, and a cotton cap.

Although there were various styles of dress, Lady Llanover, the wife of an ironmaster in Gwent, was partly responsible for the birth of a national costume. She encouraged people to wear the national dress as a way of instilling national pride at a time when the Welsh felt their identity was threatened.

The idea of a national costume was further reinforced by the work of artists who, in 1840, produced colorful prints of country costumes for the tourist trade. These prints were later developed into postcards depicting Welsh customs and costumes.

The National Musuem of Wales is located in Cardiff, and includes the Welsh Folk Museum in the castle and grounds of the neighboring St. Fagans. Here one can find out more about the natural history of Wales, and see examples of Welsh material culture, such as rural buildings.

CHRISTMAS AND NEW YEAR'S DAY

Christmas and New Year's Day are celebrated in Wales, as in many places around the world, with lots of parties, concerts, and special food.

Christmas celebrates the birth of Jesus and has been celebrated on December 25 since about A.D. 300. Christmas is an important time for Christians. Special church services are held at midnight on Christmas Eve, or early on Christmas morning when Christians celebrate the birth of Jesus by singing hymns and carols. Another tradition in Welsh churches is Christingle—the practice of carrying oranges with lighted candles in them. The orange symbolizes the world and the candle symbolizes Jesus, the light of the world.

In Wales Christmas is called *Y Nadolig* ("NAH-doll-ig"), and, in some parts, it is the custom to rise early on Christmas morning to attend a church service, called *Plygain* ("PLIG-in"), which means daybreak, held between 3 and 6 a.m. *Plygain* is anything from a short morning service during which carols are sung by visiting soloists to a service lasting up to 9 a.m. with as many as 15 carols.

Welsh child unwrapping presents on Christmas morning.

The service is often followed by a day of feasting, a standard Christmas dinner consisting of stuffed turkey, roast potatoes, and vegetables. In some places, it is toasted bread and cheese, called Welsh rarebit, which is washed down with ale. Most people spend Christmas Day with their families and welcome in New Year's Day with their friends. The new year is seen as a fresh start and a break from the past. People often try to finish off any business from the last year and make New Year's Day resolutions.

EASTER

Easter is another Christian festival, this one coming in the beginning of spring. It is a time for families, feasting, and Easter eggs. The egg is an ancient symbol of reawakening that was adopted by the Christians to represent the Resurrection. In North Wales and Anglesey, children used to go around the neighborhood collecting eggs, rattling clappers (generally used for scaring birds), and chanting rhymes as they made their rounds. Once collected, the eggs were painted and hidden outdoors for an egg hunt. Such age-old customs are far less common now that chocolate Easter eggs have been added to the Easter festivities.

Good Friday or *Gwener y Groglith* ("GWEN-er groglith") is a solemn day when Christians remember the crucifixion of Christ. Many churches hold services which are stripped of flowers and other adornments, and the church bells are silent.

Easter Sunday is a very important day to Christians because it is the day when Christ resurrected from the dead. Celebrated on the first Sunday after the full moon following the spring equinox on March 21, the mood is more cheerful with flowers and church bells. Before sunrise on the joyous Easter Monday or *Llun y Pasg* ("THEEN-pasg"), crowds climb to the highest point in the area to watch the sun "dance" as it rises to honor the resurrection of Christ. In Llangollen, in the Vale of Clwyd, villagers used to greet the arrival of the sun's rays on the top of Dinas Bran with three somersaults. A basin of water was also carried to catch the reflection of the sun "dancing."

Hot cross buns are traditionally eaten on Good Friday—the cross commemorating the crucifixion of Christ. The Welsh believe that bread baked on Good Friday will never get moldy because a kind woman gave a loaf of bread to Jesus on the day he was crucified.

Another festival is Remembrance Day, which commemorates those who died in World Wars I and II. On and before Remembrance Sunday, the closest Sunday to Armistice Day on November 11, the Welsh give money to charities and wear poppies.

MAY DAY BANK HOLIDAYS

The first Monday of May is traditionally a holiday to celebrate spring's arrival. In the past everyone collected green branches to decorate their houses, and danced around a Maypole presided over by a May Queen. There are still Mayday celebrations in many parts of Wales, such as Cardiff, where the celebration includes Maypole dancing, music, clowns, carnivals, food, and drink.

Britain owes its bank holidays to Sir John Lubbock, a Member of Parliament and, not surprisingly, a banker. Lubbock believed that there should be more statutory vacations to ease the burdens of the working class. In 1871 he managed to pass the Bank Holidays Act in parliament. This forced all banks to close on the first Monday in May, and because there were no banking facilities, other employers had to close on that day as well. Additional legislation followed, giving Britain more bank holidays. Most Welsh like to take a short break at the seaside during these occasions.

WELSH PUBLIC VACATIONS

New Year's Day (*Nos Galan*), January 1
St. David's Day, March 1
May Day Bank Holiday, first Monday in May.
Spring Bank Holiday, last Monday in May
Easter Monday (*Llun y Pasg*), moveable feast
Good Friday (*Gwener y Groglith*), moveable feast
Summer Bank Holiday, last Monday in August
Remembrance Sunday, closest Sunday to November 11
Christmas Day (*Y Nadolig*), December 25
Boxing Day (*Gwyl San Steffan*), December 26

HALLOWEEN

An example of a festival which is not a public holiday is Halloween on October 31. Associated with the supernatural, this is celebrated with bonfires, candles, and sometimes fireworks. Children dress up as witches and ghosts, and go around the neighborhood asking for candy. A popular game is apple bobbing. Apples are placed in a large bowl of water on the floor. They then try to pick up an apple only with their teeth. Another custom is for a young man to walk around the churchyard a few times at night wearing his coat and vest inside out and reciting the Lord's Prayer backwards. This courageous youth then puts his finger through the keyhole of the church door to prevent any spirits from escaping. It was once believed that the apparitions of those who would soon die could be spied through the keyhole. In more rural areas, young men dress up in sheepskins and old ragged clothes and blacken their faces. After chanting weird rhymes, they are given gifts of apples, nuts, or beer.

Two children dressed up as witches stand in front of a Halloween pumpkin.

FOOD

WELSH COOKING IS SIMPLE and wholesome. Milk, butter, cheese, and oats are common to many recipes, as is lamb. Traditional cooking techniques include roasting, simmering, and baking on a griddle. There are many tasty dishes such as roasted lamb with herbs, savory pies, hearty stews, cakes, and steamed puddings.

MEALS

Meals can be confusing in Wales. The food, the time it is eaten, and what the meal is called vary throughout the country. The description below is a generalization.

Most Welsh people start the day with a light breakfast of tea and toast or cold cereal. When it is cold outside, they might eat hot oatmeal, a

Left: **The menu of a Welsh café.**

Opposite: **Pastry shop in Betws-y-coed.**

favorite in many parts of Great Britain. Some people might have a cup of tea or coffee, and a cookie or a piece of cake around 11 a.m. On the weekend they might have a traditional "fry-up." This is a full breakfast of fried eggs, bacon, sausages, bread, and perhaps tomato, which is washed down with lots of tea.

Lunch is usually eaten at 1 p.m. If it is a main meal, it may be called dinner. But in the cities it is more common for people to eat a quick sandwich at lunch and their main meal in the evening at 6 or 7 p.m. Depending on which part of Wales you are in, this may be called dinner, supper, or tea. The meal might consist of meat, fish, or a stew, and is usually eaten with potatoes and a vegetable.

Welsh people do not eat out nearly as often as Americans do, but there are some typical eating places that they frequent every day. Besides pubs, people might eat in a café during the day. Sometimes called workman's cafés, these eating places offer cheap, filling meals in a relaxed atmosphere. After a long day at work, some people might prefer a quick "take away" of fish and chips or Chinese food. Fast food has also found its way to Wales. It has become commonplace for cities such as Cardiff have McDonald's and Pizza Hut outlets.

DRINKS

Although there are a few independent breweries and one or two companies making Welsh whiskey, on the whole, Wales does not produce much alcohol. The Welsh still drink lots of tea, coffee, and soft drinks, but are not exactly teetotallers. The average Welshman enjoys his beer, which is very much the national drink of Wales. Although beer is the most popular alcoholic drink, wine is becoming more commonly drunk throughout Great Britain. Country wines, made from wild flowers and weeds, and ginger beer are also popular in Wales. At Christmas some people drink mead made from fermented Welsh honey, and mulled wine, which is a type of spiced wine.

Below: **Welsh family enjoying some wine during the Christmas festivities.**

Opposite: **Fish and chips comes, typically, wrapped in newspaper and served with salt and vinegar.**

PUBS

The pub (short for "public house") is an institution throughout Great Britain, and Wales is no exception. The pub is an informal place where people can meet, share a drink, and have a chat. In the old days pubs served nothing but beer and spirits, but these days they serve coffee, tea, and hot food. There are no waiters in a pub, and if you want to eat or drink something, you have to go and get it yourself at the bar.

People go to the pub quite regularly and will often step in for a quick drink after work. The pub owner knows most of his customers personally and often chats with the regulars. In Wales even a stranger can enjoy a conversation with a pub owner. And if he happens to be busy serving customers, there is usually a charming Welsh person with whom you can strike up a conversation!

BEER

There is a tradition of brewing beer at home, one that still persists in rural Wales. In the 19th century farmers brewed beer for their workers, who expected beer or cider with their meals. Most social occasions such as weddings, christenings, and even funerals were observed with plenty of beer. In the 19th century brewing became large scale, and the bigger foreign breweries came to South Wales to supply beer to thirsty miners, steel, and dock workers. The Welsh like English beers and bitters but still prefer their own brews. "Brains" is the locally brewed beer in Cardiff.

A local savoring some beer at a pub in Cardiff.

Sheep being rounded up on a farm in the Cambrian Mountains.

FOOD

Typical Welsh cuisine includes dishes such as roast meats, pies, cakes, jams, and puddings. Many of the dishes have simple ingredients. Dairy herds are in abundance in Wales, so it is no surprise that traditional cooking methods use lots of milk, butter, and cheese. The best known cheese is Caerphilly cheese, which used to be a lunchtime favorite of the miners. Welsh rarebit is a traditional snack eaten throughout Wales. There are two ways to make it. You can toast a slice of cheese on bread or pour a mixture of milk, cheese, eggs, and ale over toast.

Lamb features in many recipes. It can be roasted with cider and rosemary, stewed with potatoes and leeks, or cooked with scraps of vegetables in a broth. Lamp and mutton pies are also popular in Wales.

Wales is also a fish lover's paradise. Fine salmon and trout are caught in the rivers, and cockles are gathered from the sands along the coastline. Many of the coastal towns used to be busy ports, and there are still good catches of cod, sole, and lobster.

LAVERBREAD

Laverbread (sometimes called Welsh caviar) or *bara lawr* ("BAR-ah lah-war") is a delicacy in Wales. It is edible seaweed that is processed into a greenish black gelatin. Since the seaweed grows on coastal rocks along the beaches, from which it is harvested by hand, the supply of laverbread tends to be erratic as heavy swells occasionally cover it in sand and it cannot be easily gathered. Unprocessed algae is also eaten by North Americans and northern Europeans, and known as dulse in Canada and the United States and dillisk in Ireland.

Laverbread is very popular in South Wales. It is rich in minerals and vitamins and was once eaten by miners who worked underground because it helped to combat vitamin deficiencies stemming from a lack of sunshine and fresh air. Laverbread used to be sold door-to-door by women who carried packets of laver in big baskets. Now it is sold in supermarkets and specialty shops. Laverbread can be served coated with oatmeal and fried with bacon or made into a sauce to accompany fish or mutton.

BARA LAWR

1 lb. (45g) fresh lawr
1 lb. (45g) medium or fine oatmeal
salt and pepper
3/4 oz. (85/113g) bacon fat

Soak the laver in water for a few hours to remove the sand and salt. Simmer in hot water for several hours, breaking up the laver with a spoon. Mix the puree with oatmeal, salt, and pepper. Shape into small cakes (1/2-inch, 2.5/5-cm thick), cover with oatmeal, and fry with bacon fat. Serve with grilled meat.

The diet of the past was frugal but tasty. Farmers, miners, and factory workers needed nourishing food that could be prepared quickly at the end of the day. In North Wales a popular harvesting snack was a dish called siot *("SHOT"), made by soaking oatcakes in buttermilk. In South Wales a favorite dish at lunchtime was* sucan *("SOOK-an"), a cold sour grain soup.*

Welsh cheese, bread, and jam make a quick and easy picnic meal.

SWEET SENSATIONS

There are all sorts of pastries and bread in Wales. Currant bread or *bara brith* ("BAR-ah breeth") is spicy, speckled fruit bread made from flour, yeast, and currants that have been soaked overnight in tea. Crumbly Welsh cakes are baked on a griddle, served with sugar, and laden with dried fruit and spices. These are teatime favorites that used to be served to tired travelers at inns before supper. Oatcakes and pancakes made with buttermilk are also popular, as are currant buns and bread pudding. Honey, apples, and soft fruits such as berries grow well in the south and the Welsh know just how to preserve them as jams and jellies to spread on toast, or as chutneys for meat.

In some parts of North Wales, toffee-making parties used to be a traditional part of Christmas and New Year's festivities. A light supper would be followed by games, story telling, and the making of toffee. The toffee mixture would be boiled and then poured onto a stone slab. The guests would then butter their hands, peel off the toffee, and eat it.

Welsh lamb has a delicate flavor developed through slow maturing on natural pastures. On Sundays many families get together to enjoy a hearty lunch, known as the Sunday lunch. This is a big meal of roast lamb served with potatoes and gravy, followed by a dessert such as apple pie or pudding.

ROAST LAMB

1–2 lb. (900g) rack of lamb, skinned and chilled
2 cloves of garlic, crushed with salt
2 tablespoons of honey
1 pint (150ml) of dry white wine
salt
black pepper, freshly ground
1 tablespoon of fresh rosemary

Score the thin layer of fat covering the lamb into a diamond pattern. Combine the crushed garlic, honey, wine, seasonings, and rosemary and marinate the meat in this mixture for 30 minutes. Place the lamb on a wire rack above a roasting pan. Pour the juices from the marinade over the meat and let them drip through into the pan below. Roast in a hot oven at 425°F (220°C) for 30 minutes, or a little longer if you do not like your lamb pink. Serve the lamb in slices.

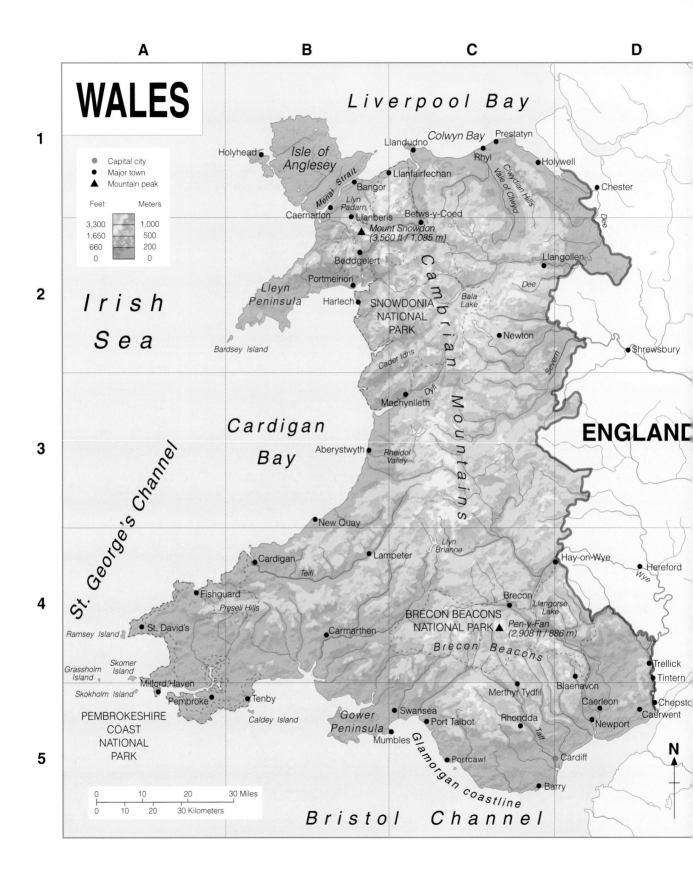

WALES

A   **B**   **C**   **D**

Liverpool Bay

1

- Capital city
- Major town
- ▲ Mountain peak

Feet	Meters
3,300	1,000
1,650	500
660	200
0	0

Holyhead

Isle of Anglesey

Llandudno · *Colwyn Bay* · Prestatyn
Rhyl · Holywell

Llanfairfechan

Bangor

Menai Strait

Llyn Padarn

Caernarfon · Llanberis · Betws-y-Coed

▲ *Mount Snowdon (3,560 ft / 1,085 m)*

Clwydian Hills
Vale of Clwyd

Chester

Dee

Llangollen

2

Irish Sea

Beddgelert

Portmeirion

Lleyn Peninsula

Harlech

SNOWDONIA NATIONAL PARK

Bardsey Island

Cambrian

Bala Lake

Dee

Newton

Shrewsbury

Cader Idris

Cardigan Bay

Machynlleth

Dyfi

Mountains

Severn

3

Aberystwyth

Rheidol Valley

ENGLAND

St. George's Channel

New Quay

Lampeter

Llyn Brianne

Cardigan

Teifi

Hay-on-Wye

Hereford

Wye

4

Fishguard

Preseli Hills

Carmarthen

BRECON BEACONS NATIONAL PARK ▲ *Pen-y-Fan (2,908 ft / 886 m)*

Brecon · *Llangorse Lake*

Ramsey Island

St. David's

Brecon Beacons

Trellick

Skomer Island

Grassholm Island

Milford Haven

Pembroke

Tenby

Skokholm Island

Caldey Island

PEMBROKESHIRE COAST NATIONAL PARK

Gower Peninsula

Swansea
Port Talbot

Mumbles

Merthyr Tydfil

Rhondda

Taff

Blaenavon

Caerleon

Newport

Tintern

Chepstow

Caerwent

Portcawl

Cardiff

Barry

Glamorgan coastline

N

5

0	10	20	30 Miles
0	10	20	30 Kilometers

Bristol Channel

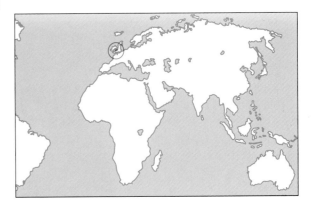

QUICK NOTES

OFFICIAL NAME
Principality of Wales

LAND AREA
8,016 square miles (20,768 square km)

CLIMATE
Maritime climate. Rainfall is frequent; annual average: 55 inches (1,397 mm). Annual mean temperature: 50°F (10°C)

HIGHEST POINT
Mount Snowdon (3,561 feet/1,085 m)

NATIONAL PARKS
Snowdonia, Pembrokeshire Coast, Brecon Beacons.

AREAS OF OUTSTANDING NATURAL BEAUTY
Gower Peninsula, Lleyn Peninsula, Isle of Anglesey, Clywdian Range, Wye Valley

MAJOR LAKES
Bala, Llangorse

MAJOR RIVERS
Dee, Severn, Wye

ISLANDS
Anglesey, Bardsey, Caldey, Grassholm, Ramsey, Skokholm, Skomer

CAPITAL
Cardiff

COUNTIES
Clywd, Dyfed, Gwent, Powys, Gwynedd, Mid Glamorgan, South Glamorgan, West Glamorgan

POPULATION
2.9 million (1997)

OFFICIAL LANGUAGES
Welsh, English

MAJOR RELIGION
Christianity. The majority being Protestant and non-conformist. Roman Catholicism is a growing minority.

CURRENCY
The pound sterling. 1 pound = US$1.45 (as of September 1, 2000)

FLAG
White and green horizontal stripes with a red dragon in the center.

WELSH NATIONAL EMBLEMS
The leek, a vegetable with a cylindrical bulb and leaves; and the daffodil, a plant with yellow flowers with a trumpetlike corona.

IMPORTANT HOLIDAY
St. David's Day (March 1), to commemorate the patron saint of Wales

IMPORTANT CULTURAL EVENT
Royal National Eisteddfod

GLOSSARY

bara brith ("BAR-ah breeth")
Currant bread.

bara lawr ("BAR-ah lah-war")
Also called Welsh caviar. It is edible seaweed processed into a greenish black gelatin.

bard
Celtic singer or the winner of a competition at an *eisteddfod*.

Celt
Gaul or member of Celtic-speaking peoples.

coracle
A small, oval, rowing boat made of skins or tarred or oiled canvas stretched on a wicker frame.

crwth ("CROOTH")
Old Welsh stringed instrument, four of its six strings played with a bow, two plucked by the thumb.

Cymru ("COME-ri")
Welsh word for Wales.

druid
A priest among the ancient Celts of Great Britain, Gaul, and Germany; or an *eisteddfod* official.

eisteddfod ("ACE-deth-vord")
A competitive congress of Welsh bards and musicians.

gorsedd ("GOR-seth")
A meeting of bards and druids.

gwyniad ("GWIN-yad")
A whitefish found in Bala Lake.

Industrial Revolution
The social and economic changes resulting from the mechanization of industry that began in England about 1760.

Mabinogion
The title of four tales in the *Red Book of Hergest*, a Welsh manuscript of the 14th century.

Neolithic
Characteristic of the last phase of the Stone Age, from 9,000 to 8,000 B.C.

non-conformist
A Protestant separated from the Church of England.

Plygain ("PLIG-in")
A church service on the morning of Christmas.

pub
Slang word for public house, which is an inn or tavern.

S4C
Sianel Pedwar Cymru or Channel Four Wales.

Welsh rarebit
Welsh dish of toasted bread and cheese.

BIBLIOGRAPHY

Boyes, V. *The Druid's Head*. Llandysul, Wales: Gomer Press/Pont Books, 1997.

Ifans, R. *The Magic of the Mabinogion*. Talybont, Wales: Y Lolfa, 1993.

Jones, M. & J. Spink. *Are you talking to me?* Llandysul, Wales: Gomer Press/Pont Books, 1994.

Lowson, N. *A New Geography of Wales*. Cambridge, England: Cambridge University Press, 1991.

Sheppard-Jones, E. *Stories from Welsh History*. Ruthin, Wales: John Jones Publishing, 1998.

Thomas, D. *A Child's Christmas in Wales*. London, England: Orion Publishing Group Ltd., 1993.

The Welsh Books Council also has a useful website: www.wbc.org.uk.

INDEX

INDEX

INDEX

PICTURE CREDITS
ANA: 11
Archive Photos: 36, 85
Dave G. Houser: 42, 74, 112
David Simson: 58, 61, 63, 64, 79, 113, 118, 120
Focus Team: 121
Hulton Getty Picture Library: 26, 27, 29, 34, 93, 106
International Photobank: 6, 7, 12, 18, 23, 35, 48, 59, 72, 88
John R. Jones: 3, 4, 5, 10, 13, 14, 16, 17, 19, 40, 41, 43, 44, 45, 46, 49, 52, 56, 65, 66, 67, 69, 80, 82, 83, 89, 91, 92, 101 (top), 102, 103, 104, 105, 107, 123
Marshall Cavendish Archive: 109, 116
North Wind Pictures Archive: 20, 22, 24, 25, 27
Topham Archive: 95, 96, 97, 98 (both)
Travel Ink: 114
Trip Photographic Agency: 1, 9, 15, 30, 31, 32, 33, 37, 38, 39, 50, 51, 57, 62, 70, 75, 76, 77, 78, 86, 87, 90, 94, 99, 100, 101 (bottom), 108, 111, 115, 117

The author would also like to thank the following for their valuable assistance:

The Welsh Book Council
The Museum of Welsh Life
The National Assembly for Wales
The University of Wales (Welsh Department in Aberystwyth)